FROM DESPONDENCY TO AMBITIONS: WOMEN'S CHANGING PERCEPTIONS OF SELF-EMPLOYMENT

To Malcolm and Biggi

From Despondency to Ambitions: Women's Changing Perceptions of Self-Employment

Cases from India and other developing countries

USCHI KRAUS-HARPER

Routledge
Taylor & Francis Group

LONDON AND NEW YORK

First published 1998 by Ashgate Publishing

Reissued 2018 by Routledge
2 Park Square, Milton Park, Abingdon, Oxon, OX14 4RN
711 Third Avenue, New York, NY I 0017, USA

Routledge is an imprint of the Taylor & Francis Group, an informa business

Publisher's Note
The publisher has gone to great lengths to ensure the quality of this reprint but points out that some imperfections in the original copies may be apparent.

Disclaimer
The publisher has made every effort to trace copyright holders and welcomes correspondence from those they have been unable to contact.

A Library of Congress record exists under LC control number: 98071965

ISBN 13: 978-1-138-31961-5 (hbk)
ISBN 13: 978-0-429-45380-9 (ebk)

Contents

Acknowledgements

Many people have helped me to put together this book, and I am forever grateful to them: Professor Sue Birley of the Management School of Imperial College, London, supervised the original research that eventually led to this book; colleagues at Cranfield School of Management gave intellectual support in designing the typology; colleagues and friends at Xavier Institute of Management in Bhubaneswar enabled me to find the four communities where I conducted the original field research; particularly Biraj Laxmi Sarangi and Suchitra Pradhan helped me to understand ways of life of the women and men of Orissa and Swapna Harrison was such a good translator and interpreter, explaining the meaning of many customs and words to me.

I also want to thank all those women and men, with whom I have worked throughout the last ten years in so many development programmes, and who have helped me to collect many of the stories included in this book. Among them are Fauziah Pavan from Malaysia, Namukolo Musonda from Zambia, Njoki Kiruthu from Kenya, Baboucarr Jobe from The Gambia, and particularly Kadambini Bhuyan, Sasi Prabha and Sister Neomi Pinto from India, who have been wonderful, inspiring friends and who have opened my eyes to many critical issues of poverty and 'women's development'.

Participants in training programmes have been a source of ideas and many have been willing to share their views on my typology. I am grateful particularly to Joyce Assanga, Manjushree Das, Pratiba Das, Namita Datta, Aneeta Dutta, Azizul Hoque, Sheela Joseph, Biggi Kraus-Schmitz, Valsala Kumari, Wambui Mboche, Amitabh Mishra, Mahfuz-Ara Miva, Beatrice Odiyo, Anuradha Saxena, Rajiv Sinah and Sandra Wanduragala; their discussions during a workshop at Xavier Institute of Management in Bhubaneswar in 1995 have resulted in the list of characteristics of an empowered woman, which is presented in the last chapter of this book.

And I thank Malcolm, my husband! Ten years ago I told him, that I would never want to be a 'women's woman'; he nevertheless invited me to contribute to a programme for women entrepreneurs in Zambia, that entirely changed my beliefs. He was also a critical proof-reader, and his suggestions and constant encouragement have been crucial in finalising this book.

My greatest thanks goes to all the many women this book is about. Without their willingness to cooperate, to tell their stories and to talk to me again and again, this book would not have been possible.

1 Introduction

What this book is about

This book is about poor women, and whether and when they see self-employment and enterprise as a desirable and feasible solution to the economic and social difficulties they find themselves locked into. It is also about change, about how change has come to some women, and why it has not come to others.

And it is a personal expression of disquiet which I know is shared by many other people; disquiet about whether the many income generation projects and micro-enterprises that are promoted for women in the so-called developing countries are achieving anything that has a positive, *lasting* impact on the lives of people, especially women who live in poverty. Poor women - and men - need 'careers'[1] as much, if not more, as the non-poor. The destruction or degradation of their traditional vocations and occupations through the process of industrialisation and accumulation, and the lack - or rather inaccessibility - of suitable alternatives and choices, is one of the most fundamental problems of poverty. Micro-enterprise is a risky alternative; it can only be a passing solution unless it has a fair chance to grow into something more substantial that can provide an adequate[2] income. Most women do not - for various reasons discussed throughout this book - want to run larger enterprises, even if they could, but if their micro-activities can not provide that adequate income and enough surplus to put something aside for 'rainy days', the women are bound to remain where they are now: in poverty.

This book is not based on statistical evidence, on representative samples or statistical correlations. It is based on the stories that women have told me, on personal notes of interviews, visits and observations, collected over many years in many countries, but particularly over the last five years in India. It it is more than a journalistic account of the lives and work of women, because I have added a more systematic analysis of all this data and have developed 'types' which help to bring out some essential topics.

I hope that this book will be read by teachers and students of development and of gender studies, and by development planners and practitioners, who want to assist women on their way out of despondency and, ultimately, out of poverty.

1

Guide to the book

*   In this introductory **Chapter One** I briefly describe the background against which this book was written: Especially in poor communities men's low income alone is not sufficient, or not reliable enough, to secure better living conditions for their families. Development aid has discovered the importance of women's economic contributions, and is beginning to recognise women's need for, and right to, economic independence. But there are not enough employment opportunities, and self-employment and enterprise are seen as an alternative. Women's income generating programmes and projects are promoted everywhere but the impact of these efforts is not very encouraging. We need to listen to women, they may have different agendas and different measurements of success.

*   **Chapters Two and Three** describe five types of women; the first part of each chapter presents the case of a typical woman; the second part of each chapter discusses the peculiarities of the type, using examples of women from across the world to highlight specific issues:

    Chapter Two: Some of the women I met seemed to have lost - or never had - heart or hope. They belonged to very poor families or lived alone with their small children, and often did not have enough money to be able to have at least one decent meal a day; but they said they did not want to or could not do any business - or anything else - because they did not know anything, could not think of anything, nor concentrate on anything. Some of them said that to be poor "is our destiny", and most of them were generally negative about their own skills and abilities. The negative attitude towards self-employment or enterprise does not spring from negative experience with enterprise but from oppression, from a general feeling of despair or powerlessness. These women are caught in what has Chambers has called the 'deprivation trap',[3] hindered by poverty and by their gender. I have called them the *negative-despondent* women.

    Other women would like to do 'something' to earn an income; but this 'something' is not quite clear. They would like to generate income on a self-employed basis but are not sure whether they can do it, or do not know what to do. There are some who say that they cannot "go out" because they are women; there are others who would do something "if somebody would provide assistance" or "if somebody would give the money to start". They are ambivalent about self-employment as a better way of earning an income, but it is something that they keep as a possibility in the back of their mind. They are the *uncertain* women.

Chapter Three: Most women can be called 'enterprising' in the way I will introduce the concept later in this chapter. But their enterprising activities are of different qualities and consequences.

Two types of enterprising women are pragmatic; they are realistic, concerned with practical results, in their inclination to enterprise:

A few women among the enterprising women had a negative view of enterprise. These women are 'lucky' enough to have found wage work as cleaners, house-helpers or day-labourers and they do not want to earn income in any other way although the work is badly paid; they are very realistic about their possibilities and their attitude goes with the proverb "a bird in the hand is worth two in the bush". They do not believe that they can start any enterprise which would give them the same kind of income. These are the women with a *negative-pragmatic* inclination towards enterprise.

Then there are women who 'just get on' with their enterprise activity. They generate self-employed income, alone or in a group, but they do it because they need money and have no other source; they would take a job or start anything different if that would bring more money. They are the *positive-pragmatic* women.

A third type of enterprising women are the *ambitious* ones. To be ambitious means to be strongly desirous *of* something or *to do* something. Among the ambitious women I met, some were not (yet) generating income from self-employment, but had a clear plan of action and were only constrained by lack of resources, usually capital. Compared with the uncertain women they did not say, for example, "if somebody would give the money" or "if somebody would tell me what to do", but they said "I can do it once I have got the money", and they were trying to convince friends, to join them or a bank to give them a loan. Some of these women also joined women's savings groups the moment they were set up, because they saw the opportunity to get access to finance. Other ambitious women I met, were generating income - from very little to quite substantial amounts- and they were investing as much effort and resources as possible in their enterprises.

• To be self-employed and enterprising is not only a matter of attitudes, but requires certain social and socio-economic preconditions. If these preconditions change, women's perceptions of, and attitudes towards, self-employment may change; development intervention can stimulate this change. **Chapter Four** shows how the five types have a transient quality and I discuss lessons, that I have learned from the women and the change, that they have, or have not, experienced.

• Are our development efforts in helping women to start enterprising activities really 'empowering'; are we, the development interventionists, empowered and able to assist others to take control of their own lives? **Chapter Five** contains some thoughts, or rather afterthoughts, because they were not there when I started the research that led to this book. I realised that we cannot help women to open their eyes and to become empowered, unless we also open our eyes to the manner, in which women forge their own ways of doing things.

• Because most of the women presented in this book are mentioned several times throughout the next chapters, the **Appendix** includes a list of all women, to make it easier for the reader to find the original case.

What should be given to the women ?

Centuries ago, a king, while travelling through his domain came across people living in dark caves. He was horrified at the gloom and ordered every family to be given lamps and oil to fuel them. Many years later, he visited the area again and found the caves in darkness. The lamps had been forgotten or were broken. The oil had run out. The king ordered more oil, new lamps. But when he returned the following year the caves were dark once more. The king summoned his minister, a wise old man, and asked for an explanation. 'Ah', said the minister, 'You gave the lamps to the men. You should have given them to the women.'[4]

*****

When I started writing this book, the UN Women's Conference in Beijing was under way and newspapers informed us, that in most countries women do more work than men and that "women are actually the breadwinners".[5] A year earlier the Wall Street Journal, certainly not a feminist publication, had found women in developing countries to be worth a first page report, saying that even the big development agencies and multilateral banks in Washington are increasingly funding women-led small businesses and farming projects "based on an assumption that women - more than men - are the critical players in the fight to relieve poverty".[6]

Some people working in 'development' have become cynical and argue that to assist women is just another development fad. I want to take a more positive view and assume, that people in decision making positions in development institutions are a bit like the king in the story: Their intentions to alleviate and ultimately to abolish poverty are well-meant, but more often than not hasty, not well thought through, lacking understanding, not prudent. It takes time to 'understand', it is a slow process of trial and error as it involves human beings on both ends of the understanding.

It has taken a long time for 'development experts', and even longer for the general public, to recognise the strengths of women in developing countries. I suppose I am one of these 'experts'; it took me twenty years to understand that the Miriam Martinez of my teenage years in Colombia in the 1960s, with her enterprising activities - of which I shall talk later - was not an isolated phenomenon but part of a global reality. It needed twenty enterprising women in Zambia to set off in me a process of understanding, of realising the importance of women's enterprise.

The discussions initiated during the   UN decade for women (1975-1985) led to many 'women in development' programmes, and researchers began to look into all manner of 'women and development', and later 'gender and development' issues. Slowly, development workers and planners became aware, that it is often the poor woman herself, and not so much her husband, who is investing in change for a better livelihood for her family. Many studies confirm that poor families depend on the economic productivity of a woman, because women are the main earners in an increasing number of households, and women contribute a larger share of their earnings to basic family maintenance. We now know that increases in women's income translate directly into better child health, nutrition and education.[7]

And there has been another set of learning: In the course of the last fifteen years governments and international agencies increasingly became aware of the importance of what is called the 'informal sector'. It is in this sector that women's economic activities are mostly to be found; in the long run no development programme, however male-biased, could therefore fail to notice these women and accept, and sometimes even promote them as what they have always been: 'active players' in the development process.

When something new is discovered, at the beginning there is often a great deal of enthusiasm and hopes. This is also true for 'the informal sector' and 'women's enterprise': there are exaggerated expectations of what self-employment, micro- or small enterprise promotion - through training or provision of credit - can do to improve poor women's (and poor men's) lives. I have experienced this enthusiasm at international conferences, during field assignments in several countries, and while teaching short course participants from many countries in the United Kingdom and elsewhere. At least ninety-five per cent of the 250 odd government and non-government organisations that have sent participants to courses on which I have taught during the last eight years, promote or run small-enterprise or income generating activities for women. The impact of their efforts is in many cases questionable, to say the least.

On the whole, programmes to promote women's income generating activities have not been very successful and, still less, sustainable. Many of the projects aiming to 'empower' women, often using income generating activities as one major point of entry, have failed to do so. 'Their' women may earn a bit more money as a result, but are entirely dependent on the goodwill and efforts of the development organisation. Others offer training programmes for women to set up enterprises, but a large majority of the women who succeed, are the ones who would have succeeded anyhow, although maybe more slowly. These women often come because attending the training programme is a means, sometimes a must, to get a loan.

A few excerpts from my diaries and field notes illustrate this. For many years I have kept such diaries and notes about my work. It began in 1965 when, still a student, I was asked to translate for a group of journalists who had come to the inauguration of one of the very first development projects of German aid. But it took twenty years from then to my own discovery of women, and to understand that my first development experience was not an isolated incident, but an approach to development: men received training, women received welfare. Twenty years later women came 'into fashion' and there was money to be made out of poor women.

Colombia 1965: The Governor of the Departmento del Atlantico inaugurated a technical training centre financed by the German Development Aid Agency (GAWI)[now GTZ]; the first group of young men is already being trained here in metal-works. Later we visited a welfare programme for mother and child care and old widows initiated by a group of women, including wives of the German technicians of the GAWI project.

Cabo Verde 1975: The people of the aid coordinating office took us to see other development activities; one of these was a women's tailoring cooperative. It was sad to see how of the ten or so sewing machines, given to this project by a Belgian group, eight lay idle because the women had great difficulties to sell their products.

Tanzania 1976: Yesterday evening I was asked to come to a place where a women's group had set up a knitting workshop. They had been given two knitting machines by a German voluntary organisation, but both machines had broken down some time ago and nobody here knew how to repair them; they were hoping I did - but I did not.

Zimbabwe 1989: The organisers of a conference on women's entrepreneurship took us conference participants to visit women's enterprises; we drove quite a long time to see, among other similar things, a nursery run by a quite well-to-do middle class woman and a women's handicrafts group. It was not quite clear what the women were actually doing apart from producing antimacassars of dubious quality. There did not seem to be much demand for these products.

The Gambia 1993: Although a large proportion of the population of The Gambia live in and around Greater Banjul, and the markets are full of women, in order to see 'enterprising women' we were driven about one hour to a village on the other side of the river.   The NGO[8] (one of the largest and most reputable ones) had once run a training programme there for one of 'their' women's groups, teaching them how to make tomato puree. One woman took us to a shed and showed us the pots and other utensils they had used for the workshop. Are they not in use now? No, she said, we don't have time.

The next day we went to see two women gardening groups 'belonging' to another NGO. It turned out that the garden 'projects' had nothing to do with the NGO; it is quite common practice for women in The Gambia to use common land for gardening vegetables. What the NGO seemed to be trying to do was to turn these women into 'their' groups by initiating savings and credit activities. One needs to have women's groups if one wants to attract donor money these days... .

Malaysia 1994: Another needs assessment study of women in the food processing sector, this time in Malaysia: The women of a government department took us to see three of 'their' enterprising women's groups: Of the three groups visited, only two were actually processing food; the third visited place turned out to a large, private vegetable garden of one member of a group, the other members were obviously not involved in anything at the moment.

The other two groups turned out to be private enterprises. One of these enterprises was employing twelve members of the village women's group, all initially processing food individually and on a tiny scale; their employer was a group member. They produced several types of savory and sweet snack food, working in two shifts in a rather small shed. The demand is higher than their production capacity, which is limited by production space, equipment and "committed workers".

We were told that the members of the second group have several individual activities: vegetable garden, production of spices, production of pickles and chili sauces. Yet we went to see only one member of that group: a woman who cultivates oyster mushrooms, earning an income of M$ 800 on average per month; her second business is catering for the local school from which she earns another M$ 800; she works from home, using her kitchen for the preparation of food, and a garden shed for the cultivation of mushrooms. She had heard about mushroom cultivation on a radio programme about successful women's businesses; she managed to find out where the woman lived who cultivated mushroom so successfully, and the woman agreed to train her. None of these efforts had anything to do with the Government department.

Kenya 1994: We wanted to see *successful* women entrepreneurs who were involved in food-processing; women who were earning a substantial income, even employing people. Whoever we asked gave us the same five to six names. One of the women actually refused to be interviewed again; she had just had a TV team doing a report about her business, which had caused a lot of disruption and she could not afford more of it. Another woman I already knew from an article in a magazine published by a large Kenyan NGO.

India 1995: Yesterday and the day before K., the Indian food-technologist, and I interviewed individually some ten women, as well as three small groups of women belonging to a member cooperative of a well-known organisation for women in India. These groups were involved in food catering. The members were de-facto workers who were paid a low wage and had to shift to other units of the cooperative every three months, because otherwise they would have to be employed permanently (and thus would not let other women have a chance to earn an income - this was the argument of the organisers); none of the groups seemed to be 'empowered' to set prices for their products, or to choose the kind of food they wanted to produce and sell; they did not even know what exactly they were earning each month. We also met their supervisor, a nice middle-class lady with a degree in home-science, who was sitting in an office supervising all member cooperatives and whose directives clearly came from the executive board of the organisation. The question is: what have these women learned, that would earn them a living - apart from what they already knew - when they have to leave their work place; and what if the organisation closes down?

Thailand 1996:   We were taken to 'the field' to see enterprising women, which meant driving some forty-five minutes in a air-conditioned mini-bus at high speed to a few towns and villages in the vicinity of Chiang Mai. Some of the members of one women producer cooperative had already gathered and cooked lunch for us. After lunch we were taken first into the shop owned by the women's group, and then into another shop belonging to the chairwoman of the cooperative. Both businesses were on the same premises, openly competing with each other. Most of us did not find anything interesting and worth buying in either of them. Compared with the many similar products we had seen being sold in shops and stalls in and around Chiang Mai, the design and finish of the women's products were of lower quality.   This cooperative had received financial and other assistance through the United Nations Development Programme for about ten years.

My files are full of more such notes about women's income generating programmes, notes of interviews and observations with women's groups, individual women, programme officials and others. Not all are negative, yet it is in some ways a record of misguided, or even failed, development aid. Not many even of the more successful women are earning a decent living from enterprise because of an aid-assisted enterprise promotion or income generation programme. If they are successful, it is most often because of a combination of other factors, of which I shall talk later.

Programmes that have successfully helped women to earn a living on a reliable basis, on the other hand, are either a result of private initiative, of committed individuals or private enterprises outside the 'aid business', or of a very slow process of 'empowerment' in which a few development organisations - most often voluntary ones - have been willing to 'let go', to 'transfer power' and to build up women's capacity in the day-to-day management and in the external dealings of their enterprises.

Finding out what women want

The experience of so many programmes of doubtful success made me feel very uneasy about my work, and I knew that others shared these feelings. I decided to take a closer, more careful look at what poor women themselves think and feel about self-employment and enterprise. More than two years of field research in various communities in Orissa, one of the poorest states of

India, as well as interviews with women in other parts of India, Bangladesh, Thailand, Malaysia, Kenya, Zambia, Zimbabwe and The Gambia, and with women in England and Germany, not only provided data for this book but changed my perceptions of development, of women in general, and of enterprising women in particular.

In their book *"To the hands of the poor"* Chambers, Saxena and Shah[9] say that so many professional solutions to poverty fail because we have not given much attention to the perceptions and priorities of the poor themselves. Yes, we need to take time to listen seriously to women and to men. Much of what we will hear has been said many times before, too many times. The story that this book tells has also been told before in different ways. I still wrote it, hoping that the voices of those women in Orissa's poor communities and elsewhere may reach a wider audience.

During the time I spent in Orissa, I listened carefully to what women said, collecting their life stories, living among them for some time, watching them in their day-to-day life. During my work in other countries, I spent much time talking not only to the women I was taken to see by people from projects or training institutions I was visiting, but also to those women one can find almost everywhere along roadsides and market places, trying to make a living. In this book, I have tried to include as many as possible of the women's own quotations and stories. My own contribution is the sociological analysis, the classifying of data and categorising of the women. This is not without its problems, as it involves a process of data interpretation and reduction which can never be unbiased. Yet categories and typologies can help to highlight useful details that may otherwise get lost in the complexity of the social world.

Collecting qualitative information is never without its problems, particularly because of its 'voyeuristic' elements. This is especially true, when one is among people of a different culture, and among people who are much poorer than oneself. All the women in this book are poorer - and how I use the word poor I shall explain in the next section - than I am, many women much, much poorer. In all cases I tried to 'paid back' some of my debts to them, that is the time they have given to me, and the frankness with which they talked to me. I did so either by making contributions to their savings group or to a local project, or by helping them with house repairs, or buying their products, or just by telling them as much as they wanted to know about myself, my family and work, or other women's lives in Europe. The women are introduced by their first names only, not because of disrespect but to preserve their anonymity; the names of villages or city quarters, where given, have been changed.

Analysing what the women themselves said and did about self-employment and enterprise, and the women's immediate and wider social and economic environment, I found that these women had basically five different kind of inclinations towards enterprise. I will introduce these five types in Chapters Two and Three. The 'typical features' that are described there for each type are based on my research in India, but I have used examples from many countries, to show that women across the world share similar experiences.

I have included short cases of two European women; you may rightly ask why, when this book is to do with issues of women's poverty in so-called developing countries. But I want to make the point that women have similar coping strategies and have similar 'gender weaknesses'; I shall explain this in the following section of this chapter.

When I began the research I did not have women's inclinations or perceptions in mind; my intention was to look at their enterprising activities, to listen to their stories and to ask as many questions as possible, to learn what they were doing and how. Inclination involves issues that poor women are not asked to talk about very often: it involves considering preferences, fondness, liking; it comprises wishes and dreams. Why, one could ask, should we be concerned with poor women's wishes and dreams, when the immediate need is income for survival? But exactly because we do not ask poor people about their dreams and wishes our attempts at 'poverty alleviation' are often so dull (the term 'poverty alleviation' itself shows the poverty and cowardice of our attempts), and geared too often only to satisfy material poverty, when poverty is made up of a complex web of causes.

For those of us who are in the business of 'development', the knowledge of women's inclination towards and perceptions of enterprise is only of practical use, if we know something about the reasons for these perceptions. Development is about change; if a development intervention is, for example, to help a woman to change her negative, despondent view of herself and her own capability of earning an income from self-employment or employment, it is important to understand what has influenced it, and what has enabled other women to move out of their despondency. In other words, to understand what has opened women's eyes.

**Poor women, enterprising women and women entrepreneurs:
the problem with concepts**

Throughout many years I have met women of all social groups, classes and
castes, of all the major religions, and of many races. My concern is with the
less fortunate among these women. I call these less fortunate women 'poor
women'. I am aware, that it is very simplistic to speak of 'poor women',
when before my inner eye there appear hundreds of very different human
beings: large and small; funny and sad; depressed and happy; highly
intelligent and outright fools; tolerant and petty; kind and mean; subdued and
bubbling; black, brown, pink and yellow; workaholics and lazy madams;
'wild young things' and 'sad old crows'(note the age discrimination...); soft-
hearted comforters and ice-cold calculators. You name it. The word 'poor'
is a very broad reference to the meager means that these very different
women have at their disposition: income and assets; basic facilities; skills
that enable to express and to demand; skills that can be sold to an employer
or used to produce something that can be sold.

Most women - and men - of poor communities choose self-
employment only because they have no alternative: they desperately need
income but cannot find employment or can find only casual employment.
In one study in India[10] it was found that "... only 23 per cent of the self-
employed are 'the hard core', that is those who have the right,
'intrinsic' (inborn, ingrained) entrepreneurial motivation, and of these a
relatively lower proportion are women". This finding may matter to those
who preach and teach on 'entrepreneurship development programmes'; the
whole issue of 'intrinsic entrepreneurial motivation' is much debated in any
case. But the authors implicitly are pointing to the fact that only a low
proportion of people are self-employed by choice.

Running a micro-enterprise as a substitute for - rather than an
alternative to - employment is also called 'livelihood activity' or 'income
generating activity', the latter especially when referring to activities of
women's groups. Micro-enterprise or self-employment by choice are
sometimes also referred to as 'growth-oriented micro-enterprises'.
Livelihood activities, according to the authors of the above mentioned report,
form part of the 'survival' economy, and consist of activities into which the
woman or man is pushed for lack of more profitable alternatives. Growth-
oriented micro-enterprises, on the other hand, are potentially viable activities
into which entrepreneurs are pulled by considerations of profitability.[11]

There is an old and continuing debate about what makes an entrepreneur (or entrepreneuse); I do not believe that this debate is very important to the women I am concerned with, nor of great relevance for the kind of issues I want to cover in this book. But some readers may want to know, how I use these terms. When I speak of 'enterprising women', I mean women who are entrepreneurs *by force*, who are involved in what above has been called livelihood activities; livelihood activities I sometimes call 'enterprising activities'. And 'enterprising women' for me -and others - also include all those millions of wage workers and piece rate workers, who do not get the benefits that usually come with employment, like sick leave, or regularity of payment, or a certain degree of job security. Many millions of women, who work for one or several employers cleaning utensils or washing laundry, for example, fall into this category. The many day-labourers, women and men, are another example. Ela Bhatt, though, believes that

> "... these women are essentially entrepreneurs, if entrepreneurs are understood as individuals who assume all the risks in their business. As such, women who are economically active in the Third World are, by and large, entrepreneurs."[12]

And although Ela Bhatt is in some sense right to use the word 'entrepreneur' so broadly, I do believe, that it does make sense for some purposes to differentiate between those women who take up enterprise by force and those who do it by choice, even if the boundaries between force and choice are, as in all human actions and interaction, not clear-cut. So, when I use the term 'real entrepreneur', I use it in the same way as the authors of the report mentioned above, for those women who run growth-oriented micro- or small enterprises *by choice*.   I am not concerned with whether there are intrinsic motivations at work or whether women have been pulled into business by considerations of profitability.   But it is true that all those women "entrepreneurs" I have met in many countries who come from poor backgrounds, have chosen to go into business because they were confident, that they could earn more money that way. The issues that are of interest to me, and that I want to discuss in this book are: What in their social environment made them confident? And why are others not confident, do not even consider the possibility?

More concepts

Perceptions of desirability and feasibility

As I have mentioned earlier, becoming self-employed for most poor people in the so called developing countries is not a choice but a necessity; poverty pushes them into it. Yet throughout the next chapters I shall show how some very poor women have not taken up any income generating activity, how others prefer to work within the 'confines' of an organisation (in all cases a group activity managed by a voluntary organisation), how most take a 'positive-pragmatic' stance and how a few others have become 'real entrepreneurs'. What kind of social factors influence these different perceptions of enterprise?

During my original analysis of the large amount of information I had gathered, I came across Shapero and Sokol's [13] research about how changes in lifepath (through displacement and other factors) influence a person's perceptions of desirability and feasibility of enterprise. I borrowed these two useful concepts, as 'desirability' seemed to be an important issue in relation to the women I had interviewed: The women found certain activities to be undesirable because of customs and traditions. Other activities were or were not desirable depending on whether they could or could not be done at home; and this had to do either, again, with tradition, or was related to the women's immobility if they had small children; in other words, it had to do with their gender. 'Feasibility', or rather non-feasibility, of whatever few ideas the women had, was another constantly repeating issue.

According to Shapero and Sokol changes in the lifepath of a person are initiated through negative displacement (e.g. forcefully emigrated, fired, insulted, angered, bored, reaching middle age, divorced or widowed), being between things (e.g. out of school) or a positive pull (e.g. from a partner, mentor, customer). When the lifepath changes, perceptions of desirability and feasibility of enterprise change; these perceptions are, in turn, influenced by a number of factors such as the culture, the family, ones peers, mentors, partners, role models, demonstrations, as well as by financial and other support.

Among the women of my original sample, I found other important factors that seemed to influence their perceptions of desirability and feasibility: skills, work experience and exposure, social and artificial 'networks' (that is, voluntary or non-government organisations), availability of employment and land, and, to some extent, availability of time. I used these factors when I compared women's stories and all the other data.

Women, gender and the meaning of success

According to the *Concise Oxford Dictionary* gender is "the grammatical classification of nouns and related words, roughly corresponding to the two sexes and sexlessness"; it also gives a colloquial meaning: "a person's sex". Most people whom I have asked what gender means, did not know, but thought it had something to do with women. Gender is much more than sex, but never-the-less closely related to it in a very complex and much debated way.

In a commonly used feminist definition (which is also much taught in 'gender and development' courses), sex refers to the biological distinction between males and females, that is mainly the primary sex organs that enable men to sire, and women to conceive and breast-feed children. Sex does not change. Women have traditionally been defined by their biology (mothers) and biologically determinist theories of what women can do and cannot do, have enabled men (and women themselves) to oppress women ("women are weak, they must be protected", "women are natural carers, they are therefore best suited to look after children", etc.).

Feminists have therefore introduced the concept of 'gender', referring to the cultural interpretation of masculinity and femininity. This interpretation changes with place and time (what women and men do, what they wear, what they are allowed to say, how they are supposed to behave, differs and can sometimes be completely opposite in different cultures).

This implies that gender identity is a state of mind. Based on the knowledge of the changing pattern of gender, some feminists and others have argued that women and men are not different except for that 'little difference' which is called sex. Given the same chances, women can do exactly as men, take up occupations, develop theories, govern countries in the same way as men.

But our personal experiences suggest, that sex must have an influence on gender; we now know that some gender differences may be genetically inherited, while others are shaped by society. There will be much debate over what predominates, and what is male or female, but it is an exciting debate because it opens up chances for a more pluralistic, tolerant society.

What does this have to do with women's perceptions of enterprise and self-employment? Quite a lot. It is making us women understand that we do not need to copy men's way, that we do not need to follow men's footsteps wherever we go, be it in science, in government or in business. It means that we need to develop new frameworks for research and analysis to capture female gender. Ethnography can be a step in that direction because it can capture what Ivan Illich has called "vernacular gender",[14] because gender is always of a culture, a people; it is, unlike sex, not culturally neutral. So far we have build our understanding of the world mainly on men's perceptions, men's ways of communication: religions, science, technology have mainly been created by men. As David Morgan suggests for example Max Weber's study of the Protestant Ethic: "In this study, as in many other studies, men were there all the time but we did not see them because we imagined that we were looking at mankind".[15] What we expect from work, business, economy, what success means, is currently based on what men, predominantly white middle-class males, expect and how they measure success. It may be fit for 'genderless individuums', but such beings do not exist.

Success is a good example of the difficulty ahead; success does seem to mean something different for women than it does for men. In a study in Michigan, USA in the late Sixties (and later) Martina Horner found that women much more than men feared success because they fear negative consequences from being successful, especially in a world were success means aggressiveness and drive; women did not want to risk not being loved - especially when men had clearly expressed, that they did not want successful wives; they wanted mothers for their children. Women therefore tried their best to avoid success.[16] This picture has not changed so very much since the Sixties, especially among middle-class women and men, not only in the United States but elsewhere.

(From my diary, 1996) "We sat on the floor, forming a circle around Poonaman, a successful woman entrepreneur of Chiang Mai, Thailand. She had spread a selection of her products, blouses of different designs, in front of us and started telling her story. ... Her husband was against her business idea. "I did not pay any attention ... and I won", she said and smiled. I felt a slight uneasiness creeping in. Envy? Reproach?

Someone laughed nervously but none of us other women pursued the matter although I would have wanted to know more about this 'not paying attention'. I remembered my discussion with the girls of a tailoring class in Berhampur, India: "We cannot change it" they had said, "if women oppose, if women do not do what they are supposed to do, what their roles are in society, it will bring unrest to the family".

Yet the women presented in this book do enjoy success, many of the stories will show this. Is it because they do not aim to be 'on top', is it because they have managed to avoid being more successful than their men? Is it because they have found their 'little female corner'? Or is it that success does simply have a different meaning for most women (and some men)? I do not really know the answer; it was not the objective of my study to find this out. But I suspect that success for women involves having self-respect and being able to integrate their various 'roles' in a satisfactory manner.

What do poor women, what do most people care how we measure success, you may ask. They probably don't. But planners, policy makers, donors care; they plan for, allocate money for promoting business and other projects and programmes that can be expected to be successful. They are mostly men. They need to be aware that development, enterprise, or success may mean something different to women.

References and Notes

[1] Career means "ones advancement through life, especially in a profession", also "a profession or occupation especially as offering advancement" (see *The Concise Oxford Dictionary*, 8th ed., 1990)

[2] What is adequate will vary from place to place; it is a vague concept which I have chosen deliberately as this is not the place to discuss socio-economic indicators

[3] Chambers 1988, pages 8-9

[4] from Jung, 1987, p.123

[5] *Guardian Weekly*, September 3, 1995

[6] *The Wall Street Journal*, June 6, 1994

[7] see for example The World Bank, 1991

[8] NGO = non-government organisation

[9] Chambers, Saxena and Shah, 1989, p.7

[10] Mathew, 1995

[11] Ghate, Ballon and Manalo, 1995

[12] Bhatt, 1995, p.86

[13] see Shapero and Sokol, 1982

[14] Illich, 1983, p.3

[15] Morgan, 1981, p.93

[16] see in Dowling, 1994, pp. 154-166.

2   Handicapped by poverty and gender:
The non-enterprising women

Are there non-enterprising, poor women?

When I first got married, my mother gave me a piece of advice, which she repeated often as the years went by: "Keep your economic independence!" My mother was a housewife of the traditional kind; although she had house-helpers for much of her married life, she was never able to use her free time to earn an income. My father was of the view that "my wife does not need to work", and she succumbed to this view. It was proper not to work, especially when one had just 'arrived' at the middle classes. It was necessary to show, that the man of the house was capable, strong, powerful enough to look after his family. But although my father was a generous man, as my mother used to stress, many a time he did not agree with my mother's expressed wishes. Hence her dream of having her own income. Seventy three percent of the women I interviewed in India, Bangladesh, Zambia, Zimbabwe, The Gambia, Kenya and the UK mentioned "to be independent" as one of their reasons for having started or wanting to start a business or take up employment. Among all my female relatives, friends, acquaintances and students there is not one, who would not like to have her own income.

Not surprisingly, then, women like the ones presented in this chapter did not figure in my original ideas for the study, on which this book is based. My intention had been to find out about *enterprising* women. My awareness of the situation of the *non-enterprising* women, and my research interest in them, arose during my stay in India, where I came across many such women, many of them extremely poor, and where I started to wonder, what apart from the lack of employment opportunities and farming land hindered these women to earn any money. Of the forty women of my original sample, nineteen were not involved in self-employment; of those nineteen, one woman was begging and eight others were not generating any cash income at all. The reasons these eight women gave were:

- I don't know anything, can't do anything
- I would like to do something but don't know what (2)
- I am a woman, I cannot go out
- I have small children and nowhere to leave them (2)
- I am not allowed to go anywhere
- I am too ill to work

From a development point of view, the non-enterprising women turned out to be the most interesting group of women, but also the most difficult to understand. If they needed money so badly, why were they not, like others, involved in micro-enterprise activities, if they could not get employment? Why did they not use their time in a more productive way? They all wanted their own income, even those who did not need money so badly. Why where they so hesitant, indecisive? What was holding them back? The answer: Utter poverty and their gender.

Poverty drains body and mind

Some of the women I interviewed in Orissa, did not earn cash income in any way. Some of these women were living in utter poverty, to the extent of having to go out to beg, or maybe even become a prostitute. This means, a few of these women might have been earning cash, but they were earning it in the most humiliating way.[1]

What was happening to these women? Why had I heard so little about them? I had seen poverty before, in many places. Here it suddenly became a 'gender issue': the more one got involved in one community, the more destitute women came to the surface, so to speak.

As most research about women's income generation focuses on the women's activities and not the women themselves, it is not surprising, that in my field of work little is known about these women from very poor families, who do need income, cannot get employment but are not self-employed either, not even within a family enterprise with at least the benefit of remuneration in kind. Some of them may work very occasionally as wage workers in short-term, completely insecure occupations. Some of them, though, are too poor to work at all. And although the conventional wisdom is, that the poor, especially poor women, are endlessly struggling to make ends meet, there seems to be a point, when there is nothing to struggle with anymore.

In their discussion about "poverty and the poor" Bernstein et.al.[2] refer to a hypothesis suggested by Michael Lipton: that female participation in income-generating activities increases among the poor, but declines among the ultra-poor. To illustrate this, the authors quote a case about a family who have followed the path from poverty to ultra-poverty. Sharifa, the wife, says: "These days I have no work. If we had land, I would always be busy - husking rice, grinding lentils, cooking three times a day. ... I have nothing to do, so I watch the children and worry."[3]

Even if women find casual employment during the agricultural season, this leaves six or eight months of the year without any earnings. One of my first encounters with poor women who had nothing to do, was in a village near Bhubaneswar:

> On our way to Meena's house early this morning, we met the members of four families living in small, very low huts along a narrow lane on the outskirts of the village, were the harijan community begins. Most of the men were just leaving for work and we stopped to chat with the women and children. These are all landless, agricultural labourers; they get work during the season, the men earning twenty rupees and the women twelve to fourteen rupees a day. The men seem to get work throughout the year, although not regularly. But for the women there is only work during five months of the year. So what do they do the rest of the year? "Nothing is there to do, we sit around" said one woman and others nodded in agreement. Because most people live in extended families, there is always one woman, usually the youngest daughter-in-law, who is responsible for the cooking and much of the other household work, while the others do not seem to help much. Can't they do some joint activities, something that earns them a bit of money? The women used to have a savings fund, managed by the men, but quite soon they felt cheated by the men so they stopped saving. They have no ideas what to do with their 'idle' time. One older woman said angrily "We are poor, we don't know anything" and spat out, as if to stress her own disgust.
>
> As we walked on my friend explained to me, that poor women in these villages have a lot of spare time; they do not have land to grow vegetables or keep animals, they do not engage in any other activities. "They go to the river and gossip", she said.

Roberts Chambers talks of poor people being caught in the 'deprivation trap'. He distinguishes five categories or 'clusters of disadvantage', which interlock and reinforce each other:[4]

- *physical weakness*: refers to lack of strength, under-nutrition, poor health, physical disability and a high ratio of dependents to active adults;
- *isolation*: refers to physical remoteness, ignorance and lack of education, and lack of access to services and information;
  I would add here that it also refers to being 'remote' from ones own family and/or peers (friends, women's groups etc.) which makes particularly younger women even more vulnerable and powerless;
- *poverty*: refers to lack of income (flows of food and cash) and of wealth (stocks of assets);
- *vulnerability*: to exposure to contingencies and the danger of becoming poorer and more deprived;
- *powerlessness*: to the inability to adapt, cope and choose, and weakness in the face of exploitation and demands by the powerful.

Women more then men are caught in this deprivation trap. Robert Chambers calls this 'ascribed deprivation': certain categories of people are more likely to be poor according to ascribed characteristics such as their gender, age, membership of oppressed groups or castes.[5] In India women are significantly over-represented among the poor, however one defines poverty; women and children are the dominant subgroup among the poor, they account for 73% of the below poverty-line population.[6] Poor women's chances to generate income through employment or self-employment are, thus, not only hindered by their lack of assets, skills, and their isolation, but are also reduced by the large amount of competition for the few opportunities.

When one is very poor, one is on the bottom of the social ladder. It is not only other people's perception, it one's own realisation, as well. One is ashamed, depressed, distressed; it pulls you down. This may not be a constant condition, but it will certainly come to the surface, when one is confronted with better-off people, or in situations that expose one's poverty. This is true also for India, where people are said to be fatalistic, taking their position as God-given. Many a time women have expressed their shame and distress to me.

One day I accompanied a friend, who lives in a village and runs a small voluntary organisation there, on her weekly visit to various households. On our way we met Lata, Topan's grandmother, a woman bent and crippled by age. She was wearing an old, torn sari without a blouse and no shoes; most women here don't wear blouses or shoes, they don't have shoes and if they have one blouse, it is kept for special occasions. She was about sixty five years but she looked more like ninety. She lived with her sons. They had four little, one-room huts for four families; they were landless day-labourers. "I used to be very strong", she said "I worked hard my whole life" but "We have always been poor, always lived in broken houses". She said "broken houses", comparing mud-huts with brick houses; she is not the first to refer to her own house in this way.

A few yards further on we got to the first household my friend wanted to visit this morning. Sangita, a young woman appeared at the door of a very low, wretched looking 'broken house'. Her husband is a day-labourer but he often spends his earnings on drink, leaving his wife and two little girls without the means to buy any food; often she depends on kind neighbours to help out. The woman did not work, she has small children and nobody to look after them; there have been quarrels among the brothers and the mother-in-law, all living under one roof, one tiny room for each family. And she just had another girl three weeks ago, but the girl died after two weeks - she had probably been given too much opium, a not at all unusual way of trying to keep small children quiet during the night, in the one little room were five or more people are trying to get some sleep. She told all this in a low voice, she is shy. We sat under the dilapidated roof that stretches half a meter over a very narrow sort of porch, giving shelter from the sun but not from the great, humid heat. For a few moments none of us said anything, as if the heat had even drained our words. Then the woman spoke in a very low and fast voice to my friend: she did not have anything to offer to her guests; she was so ashamed of it. Luckily she knew my friend as someone who undertands the life of a poor woman; how awful it would have been for her, had I come alone... .

Considering all these factors it is little wonder, then, that the most severely affected women have a 'negative-despondent' attitude towards self-employment. On page 28 I will describe this type of women more in detail.

Apart from ultra-poverty there is another element at play, that hinders women from becoming economically active:

Female gender reinforces negative perceptions

Many of the women in my original sample did not generate income at all or only on a very casual basis as agricultural day-labourers. Some of these women belong to the group mentioned above, others are less despondent.

I have called these women 'positive-uncertain', because all of them had expressed a positive view of self-employment or enterprise, all of them would have liked to earn money or more money, but did not know what to do or how to do it.

Only after I had read my notes about these 'uncertain' women many times, and long after finishing the initial research, that lead to the five types of women I introduce in this book, did I realise, that the uncertain women were of a classical female gender type. Conditioned by their upbringing as girls and as the 'weaker' sex who believe - though able to take even the most extreme burden of childbirth, child-care, household and extended household work, and subsistence farming - that they are not really capable of much. And even if they have a business idea, in an interview or in a discussion with someone who they think is superior (and to this woman almost everybody else seems superior), they would be hesitant to come out with this idea, because they consider it to be too unimportant, too small to be discussed in public.

There are various interrelated forces at play in the making of the 'uncertain woman': her perception of self and of her own role, that is her perceived opportunities and constraints; and the socio-economic environment she lives in, with its norms, rules and forms of organisation and production, that is her actual opportunities and constraints.

It is beyond my knowledge, and it is also not my objective in this book, to embark on a detailed study of female psychology; especially as in this case cultural aspects would have to be taken into consideration. But so many encounters and friendships with women in many parts of the world, and the literature of and about women, have convinced me, that there are basic psychological, behavioural pattern which can be found across cultures. Where ever it may be, to be born and to grow up as a girl (or as a boy) affects the future life in similar ways, even if the degree of choices and of personal freedom will differ, not only across cultures but also across income groups within one and the same culture.

During a visit to a school in Orissa, I met a group of girls and young women, mainly school drop-outs, who were learning tailoring skills. The following is an excerpt from our revealing discussion:

.....

"If tailoring does not seem to be such a promising thing to do, why are you then here learning it?"

"I cannot get any other job, so what to do", and "At least I can stitch for the family, that saves money"

"Is it not possible to learn other skills?"

"What other choice do we have: cooking and housework, that's what we learn, that's what women do."

"Why can girls not do other things? In other countries, in other parts of India women do different jobs, have different skills which earn them an income."

"We cannot go out"

"Why not?"

"Because of the Hindu religion" and "Women involve themselves in the house; they find enough to do there"; and one girl thought "There is no courage in women!"

"What would happen if you just did it, went out to do a job, a business?"

The only married woman answered: "We cannot do that, boys are   already jobless, girls cannot go also and take jobs from them."

"Why not? Are girls less capable then boys?"

The married woman: "Girls cannot think as much as boys; also, girls will just not do it, boys have much more courage."

There followed a discussion about women's position in society here... . But the general tenor of the discussion was: "We cannot change it; if women oppose, if women do not do what they are supposed to do, what their roles are in society, it will bring unrest to the family."

In Southern Asia I often encounter disbelief when I mention, that women in Europe have problems that are similar to the ones women in Southern Asian countries have, and that these problems have similar roots: women's "fear of freedom",[7] fear of independence. In her book about "The Cinderella Complex" Colette Dowling[8] reports about a Manhattan (female) psychiatrist who "... treats many successful, upwardly reaching women; among them she has found the problem of self-constraint to be widespread. In relation to their inner abilities, too many women seem incapacitated, unable to realize their full potentials." The psychiatrist believes that fear is what holds them back:

"Women do not want to experience the anxiety that's intrinsic to the growth process. It has to do with the way they've been reared. As children, females are not taught to be assertive and independent, indeed, they are taught to be non-assertive and dependent... . Around this 'core of dependency'... develops a whole constellation of character traits which are interrelated and which reinforce each other. These traits take years to develop. As with any established character pattern, they cannot be given up without anxiety."

This then leads to what has been called 'the achievement gap': women are not achieving what they are capable of achieving, the result being an increasing gap especially between men's and women's longer-term incomes. Why is this so? Colette Dowling thinks that part of the problem are women themselves: "Women are not just being excluded from power (although that has been systematic); we are also actively *avoiding* it."   "There is no courage in women" the girls from Orissa said. Women in Orissa and in the United States seem to have more in common than some glossy magazines want us to believe.

I believe that women's fear of freedom and independence, the achievement gap, the lack of courage have a much deeper root than the socialisation of female children into women. I do not know much about the history of women's transformation from human beings with distinct but equally valid roles from men in gendered societies to the 'second sex' in a sexist society. From a few comparative observations of communities and families where subsistence production requires men and women to have clear, usually complementary tasks of equal importance, with communities where cash income is earned mainly by men selling their labour, or selling the products of their own and their family's labour, it becomes clear that much of women's misery is a product of modern economic development.[9] However, I do not wish this to be seen as a "back to the good old times" statement - for I don't believe, that those times were so good, either. But we women certainly need to be reminded of our own strengths and qualities; and that these qualities go beyond being a good mother and housewife, and that it is all right to have other ambitions.

Women's uncertainty usually reflects the outside (male) world: the kind of personal and technical skills and attitudes that are required or preferred, the requirements of time and undivided attention to do a specific job, the technical requirements such as means of transportation are often antagonistic to women's ways or at least conflicting with women's reality. If a woman can avoid the conflict she will. Women in our western societies retreat from 'powerful' jobs because, so it is said, they want to get away from the stress of the double burden. I believe it is also to do with escaping a world of miscommunication, a world that is based on male perceptions and male solutions. Women, so a Cambridge study[10] says, are more cautious, more discursive and willing to consider a range of views. That makes it more difficult for them, to work in an environment where male competitiveness prevails. That some women are happy in this male world, and some men unhappy,   only confirms that male and female are the two poles of a continuum.

Outsiders with time to spare: The negative-despondent woman

Some of the women I met seemed to have lost - or never had - heart or hope. They belonged to very poor families or lived alone with their small children, and often did not have enough money for at least one decent meal a day. Yet they said they did not want to or could not do any business - or anything else - because they did not know anything, could not think of anything, nor concentrate on anything. Some of them said that to be poor "is our destiny", and most of them were generally negative about their own skills and abilities. The negative attitude towards self-employment or enterprise does not spring from negative experience with enterprise, but from oppression, from a general feeling of despair or powerlessness. These women are caught in the 'deprivation trap'.

"If that is written in my fate": The case of Moti B.

Moti B., a young woman of about twenty-five years, lives in a small village near Bhubaneswar, Orissa, India.

The village is situated some fifteen kilometers north-east of the centre of Bhubaneswar. It lies in amongst enormous trees and extends about one kilometer along a narrow road. Paddy and vegetable fields are situated behind the houses. There is a big water-tank or pond where people used to get their water and take their baths, but some years ago two tube wells were installed and this is where the women and children now fetch the water for household purposes. Many villagers now take their bath either in the river, or in the canal that marks the eastern border of the village. There are agreed times and places for men and women during the morning and early evening hours.

According to Ms K., a woman who runs a small voluntary organisation in the village, the women prefer to go to the river where they can meet other women and 'gossip', although many of them could have their bath in their small yard.

Most of the houses are thatched mud huts, often in bad condition. Some women in the village referred to these huts as 'broken houses'. Here extended families live together under one roof. Almost all the women I interviewed here, have one room in such a 'family hut' which they share with their husband and children; each room has its own entrance and sometimes a tiny storage room. Whenever possible, cooking is done outside, sometimes there is a separate shelter which serves as a kitchen. There are a few distinctly wealthier families in the village, who own 'pukka' houses made of bricks.

Moti's village is a traditional Oriyan village. The 8,000 odd inhabitants are neatly divided into castes, each clearly distinguishable from the others by customs, ways of living and earning, even place of living. There is a sense of continuity that suggests peace - at least superficially. But according to Mrs. K., aggressive incidents between upper caste and 'harijan' people are quite frequent.

The local economy is rural, income is earned from agricultural labour, from farming and fishing, and a few government service jobs. The market place is Bhubaneswar, where farmers sell their products and where land-less men find jobs as vegetable sellers - selling small quantities of vegetables bought from farmers in the area - and as coolies during the agricultural off-season. During the dry season, jobs are also available at the various quarries along the river, where building bricks or blocks are cut out of the red, sandstone-like soil. Many harijan girls and young women work here, carrying bricks from the quarry to a collection point, earning five or six Rupees a day.

Moti's husband is a 'fisherman' by caste; in practical terms this means that sometimes he goes out to catch fresh-water fish from the nearby river; sometimes, when there is not enough fish, he buys vegetables from farmers in the village and sells them at Bhubaneswar market. He is a good father to her children, she says, but he drinks whenever he can afford it. They are very poor, all fishermen in this village are poor. Moti often does not even have enough means to prepare more than one meal a day for the five members of her family.

She was born in a small village not too far from Bhubaneswar. She was very young when she was married to the fisherman and had to move to her in-laws' house. At the beginning she used to get very homesick and go home every two to four weeks. But after her children were born she felt at home in their in-laws' house, she says. After all, a girl is taught from early childhood, that she belongs to the family of her future husband and not to the family she was born into. Now both mother- and father-in-law are dead, and she cannot afford to see her parents more than two or three times a year, because the bus-fare, although not much increased, is too expensive.

Moti, her husband and their three children aged between one and six live in one room in a small, low mud-hut. Her husband's two brothers and their families live in the same hut. Each family has one room. They are so poor, that they do not even have a little courtyard, like many of the other simple huts in the village. Nor do they have a small front or back garden to grow vegetables or to keep a few chickens.

Moti does not have much to do; in fact, another woman in the village said she is lazy. But the same applies to her sisters-in-law and other women in the village. They do not engage in any other activities but their little bit of housework. There is not much to clean, wash or cook when one is poor. The room in which Moti's family lives, measures about four by four meters; they sleep on grass-mats which are rolled up and stored in one corner during the day. In another corner is the 'kitchen', an earthen stove built into the floor, a few pots and vessels for cooking, a few tins for storage. If it rains and Moti has to cook inside, the room is filled with smoke. She does not know about smokeless cookers, nor do any of the other women in her village.

In the morning Moti and other members of her family go to collect bits of wood in the neighbourhood: twigs; small, dead branches of trees; dry bush. In the late hours of the afternoon the women and girls and small children of the family go to the river to take their daily bath together with other village women. The village men go later. Each member of the family washes her or his own clothes during this bath; even the children do, if they are old enough.

Moti, who has never been to a school, was at one time quite keen to learn something new. So when Mrs. K. asked her to join the women's 'reading group' she did. But she went only once: "My children did not want me to go, and my husband also opposed my learning to read and write".

*****

During my stay in Orissa I visited Moti's village many times, and I often met her sitting outside her little house chatting with one or the other of her three sisters-in-law. During one of these visits we had the following conversation:

"Moti, why don't you prepare and sell muri (puffed rice) like Meena does?" [Meena is another fisherman's wife living near to Moti]

"I don't know how to make muri."

"But is this not a traditional occupation of the women of your caste ?"

"Yes, but I don't know how to do it, I never learned it."

"Would you like to earn money ?"

"I don't know anything."

"But you could learn something. Why don't you join the women's group?"

"My family does not want me to go anywhere, they don't want me to learn anything."

"But what about yourself: would you like to learn something new ?"

(she shrugs her shoulders) "I don't know what; I don't have any idea."

"What about your sisters-in-law ? Can't you do something together ?"

"They don't know anything; they are just like me. We have never learned anything."

"You live in one row, under one roof. Do you share the housework like some families do ?"

"No, each family cook for themselves." [apparently there have been quarrels among the brothers]

.....

"Don't you have a dream of something you would like to do, or something that you would like to happen ?"

[she did not understand my question and Mrs. K. had to explain at length what I meant]

"I don't dream. I take care of my children, one day I will die." She shrugged her shoulders again. "Life is a misery" she said and laughed bitterly.

Seven months later: Moti's 'miserable' life has not changed. She had a lot of fights with one of her sisters-in-law; her husband has been drinking and has beaten her; she likes Mrs. K., but Mrs. K. is so busy and does not come to see her anymore. It had been so nice for her to talk to Mrs. K., there are not many 'good women' here, she said.

Four years later: Moti's situation has still not changed, with the exception that one of her children goes to the local school; the hut is still in the same condition, her husband still does the same casual work. Moti sits in front of her hut and has no dreams. "If it is written in my fate", she said, "one day things may change".

The negative-despondent woman: Determinants of a type

I have not met very many women like Moti - and I have not met any at all in Sub-Saharan Africa, which does, of course, not mean that there none - but those few seemed to have certain personal characteristics in common[11] and live under similar socio-cultural and economic conditions.

This type of woman has a negative, despondent attitude towards self-employment; she seems to have lost - or never had - heart or hope. She is very poor, her family need more income just to be able to have at least one decent meal a day. In extreme cases she survives by begging. But she does not want to or cannot do any business - or anything else - because she is negative about her own skills and abilities; "I don't know anything", "I cannot do anything", "I cannot concentrate on anything" are the kind of phrases she uses frequently to explain her situation. She does not perceive self-employment as feasible, and in extreme cases, not as desirable, although she desperately needs an income. She is likely to see the reasons for her situation in her 'fate', it is destiny and one cannot do much about it.

The negative attitude towards self-employment or enterprise does not spring from negative experience with enterprise, but from a general feeling of despair or powerlessness, or from oppression. The despondent woman is caught in the 'deprivation trap'.

> Prabha B. is such a woman; when I first met her in the slum resettlement near Bhubaneswar, where she lived with her three children were between six months and three years old, her husband (with whom she had come from another state in search of work) had left her for another woman. She was living in a one-room mud-hut with a patchy thatched roof, through which the monsoon rains came pouring in. She had once been given money by a local voluntary organisation to repair her roof, but she had used the money for other purposes. She had no skills, no other family members in reach and the money for food came from begging and possibly occasional prostitution. She did not want a part-time cleaning job that was offered to her, because where would she leave her children and furthermore she was in a state of despair, because of her roof and was not able to concentrate on anything. When we had met her the first time during the visit to the slum resettlement far outside the city, she had begged us to come into her hut and see its condition; she obviously wanted money from us. Two of the social workers of a voluntary organisation, who had come with our group to the settlement, came searching for us and wanted us to leave her house: "She is a bad woman, don't get involved with her".

The despondent woman is an oppressed or abandoned mother of small children. Her family, that is the role she has in this family, is often the reason for her despondency: if she has been abandoned by her husband, her children are dependent on her and there is no family system to support her. If there is a male head of the household, her family is not encouraging or supportive; they may even forbid her to participate in any community or income earning activities. And whatever wishes she secretly may have, the despondent woman submits to her family's demands and dictates. In a male-headed family she is a 'kept housewife' or 'kept house-helper', without any recognition of her contribution to the functioning of the family, without power and without her own means, because she is too poor even to keep a few animals or a small vegetable garden, which are the usual sources of housewives' own income.

Preeti A. is a another example of an oppressed and completely dependent young woman. She told me the following story:

"I am 20 years old. I have neither father nor mother. As little children my sister and myself stayed with our grandmother at Nuapalli, a village near Berhampur (a city in southern Orissa). They had fields and agricultural work. We never went to school; we worked as labourers and helped grandmother. Grandmother got my sister married. When grandmother died, I came to my sister's house thinking that I could help her; besides, I had no one in the village. That was 12 years ago.

At that time my sister had only one daughter. Now she has five children alive and four have died as infants. My brother-in-law does not want her to get operated because that can make her lose her health or become weak.

Getting up much before sunrise, I sweep the yard and draw rangoli [flower or other designs drawn with chalk] in front of the door and take bath. Then I light the oven and cook the food. It may be rice or suji or chapatis, and vegetables. By that time my brother-in-law and my sister are also ready. I serve the food for everyone and also feed the children. During the day my sister and I look after the children and in the evening again I do the cooking. I follow this routine every day except on days I have periods when my sister takes my place.

My brother-in-law and sister do not permit me to go anywhere. If I ask for going to meet with other girls of the colony they refuse. He has ordered me not to talk to anyone; not to look at anyone. He tells me that our fate is like this. If you begin talking to anybody, many other things will follow. So the best thing is not to mix with anyone.

Very often he has beaten me very badly. Small matters stir up his bad temper, and them he may do anything; slap me on the face, kick me, twist my hand, pinch me so as to take part of the flesh. You can see the marks of it on my thigh even now. He picked up a quarrel because the rats made a bottle fall from the top and it broke. He has only myself to blame, to beat and to kick. My sister makes some complaints about the children, about food and so on. That is enough reason for him to attack me physically and verbally.

In the last rainy season a sack of groundnut peels was left outside. We use these as fuel supplement. It was bought for us and for our next door neighbour, both sharing the cost. The sack had become wet due to rain though the peels inside were not drenched as the sack was tough and drained off the water. The neighbour complained to my brother-in-law that two ladies are idle in your house and they did not do the needful. That neighbour was a very good friend of my brother-in-law. With this, my brother-in-law got so infuriated that he beat me black and blue, first with a broom, then a metal rod. My whole body that evening was like a single wound. When my sister tried coming to my rescue he pushed her aside. Next morning my face and hands were swollen. Brother-in-law supplied medicines and injections. My sister told him then that if he only talks to that neighbour she will take poison. From that day he has not beaten me. These days he does not talk to that neighbour.

He has a shop where he melts ornaments by pouring acid and separates other metals from it and remolds the ornaments. His shop is located in Big Bazaar, in a rented room. These days his business is going down very badly. He borrows money from all sides to meet the family expenses. Life is very hard.

I feel I have so much sorrow so early in life. Long life is ahead. I do not know how to carry on living. I have to hear so much blame, insults and put up with beatings, though I live such a lonely life. When my father's mother was here for the first four years there were no beatings. I was happy. I do not think there is a way out for me from this situation. Between my sister and myself we are OK. However, she cannot help me in any way.

In my situation I am unable to make any personal plans, because if I go out anywhere without my brother-in-law's permission he will definitely put me out of the house and disown me. Then how can I live and where can I go?

It seems they are waiting that somebody might come, if that is written in my fate, and propose to marry me. I don't know whether such a day will ever come."

(Note: In Preeti's community one can find many other women of her own social class engaged in micro-business or other income-generating activities; in fact, almost every other house has some 'business' activity going on; whole families making snack food, women making paper bags or pickles or rolling papads. In other words, there are 'role models', but Preeti did not perceive them as such, did not think that she could do the same. This was mainly because the brother-in-law would not allow it, but it also reflected her personality: the insecure, fearful young woman. Other women of this type have other reasons for not getting involved in enterprising activities, but the effect is the same: *I* cannot do it).

The despondent woman has enough free time; she has, in fact, too little to do and this may add to her negative feelings about herself. Her home is tiny, most of the time she does not have enough means to cook more than one substantial meal a day, if at all, and if she lives in a rural area her family is land-less and agricultural jobs are scarce and seasonal. Because of her spare time, she may have considered the idea of becoming employed or being self-employed, but perceives it as being absolutely not feasible.

The despondent woman is illiterate and her skills are basic and related to a narrow range of domestic duties, learned from family members who also grew up in poverty. But while other women in her community may use similar 'domestic' skills to generate income, the despondent woman is not aware of her own skills and possibilities; "I do not know anything" ; "I cannot do this or that" expresses her perception.

Within her community she is isolated, and this is related to her poverty in two ways: poverty is one cause of her isolation; and isolation is a factor that contributes to poverty. She does not belong to any formal or informal 'women's group'. There may be women in her community involved in enterprising group activities, but the despondent woman is not part of it, either because her family does not want it, or because the other women reject her or do not care; she is excluded from community activities because of poverty, shame, ignorance or rejection.

If there are organisations or individuals working in the woman's community for 'change', she has not been affected by any of these organisations' activities. If she or her family have ever received outside assistance, it was financial assistance which was very soon used up to pay back debts and to buy food, in other words: to survive.

Wants to be told: The positive-uncertain woman

Most women would like to do 'something' to earn an income; but for many women this 'something' is not quite clear. They would like to generate income on a self-employed basis, but are not sure whether they can do it, or don't know what to do. There are some who said that they cannot 'go out', because they are women; there are others who would do something "if somebody would provide assistance" or "if somebody would give the money to start". They are ambivalent about self-employment as a better way of earning an income, but it is something that they keep as a possibility in the back of their mind.

"I could keep a cow": The case of Santilata D.

Santilata D. is about thirty years old. She has never been to school, but she can write her name and she is very proud of it. She is married to a day-labourer; they have two girls aged nine and seven years and a baby-girl of four months.

Santilata lives in a slum resettlement some fifteen kilometers outside Bhubaneswar. The area was settled in the late 1980 by some 8,000 squatters, who had been expelled from the city. They had migrated to Bhubaneswar from various parts of the state and elsewhere, and had been living in various slum communities, and they were often blamed for sporadic outbreaks of violence and disorder. The authorities had therefore decided to solve the problem by shifting them out of the city altogether, and had allocated an area of unused land for their resettlement. Each family was allocated a small plot of land, stand pipes were provided and electricity was made available. The people were also given building materials to construct their houses.

The people of the settlement have remained very poor, and although their housing is a little better than their old slums, they are now far away from the city where they earn or used to earn their living by casual employment, petty trading, begging, and other means.

Santilata and other women I interviewed live at one end of the settlement, in mud huts or tiny brick houses with one or two small rooms; only a handful of houses, belonging to slightly better-off people, have latrines; other people use the fields around the settlement. Each hut or house is surrounded by a tiny garden, the individual plots are not larger than 35 square meters. Some people grow a few vegetables or have one or two fruit trees; some keep a few chickens. Women go in groups to the nearby 'jungle' (bush) to collect fire wood and cow dung. Each year they have to go farther. Sometimes a woman can get casual labour at a construction site, carrying sand, and bricks. Men who work at such building sites often organise these jobs for their wives.

There is no crèche or nursery, but there is a primary school at either end of the settlement. One can also find several little stalls selling tea and paan [tiny betel leaf parcels filled with tobacco and spices], some very small food stalls for the very basic necessities, a few tailors and other workshops. A few public buses stop along the main road, taking passengers to Bhubaneswar.

The people of the settlement belong to all castes and come from various states in India. But caste does not affect their lives in the same way as it would in a traditional village. Money seems to be more important than caste, and according to the women I spoke to, one can be from a low caste but if one has money and a 'nice house', that is a brick house, upper caste people will not mind to come for a visit.

Santilata and her husband have an income of about six hundred rupees a month. The husband earns most of it, while Santilata's main occupation is to be a housewife. Sometimes she gets day-labour jobs on building sites through her husband. Then she works eight hours a day. She does this to supplement her husband's income, to maintain the family. She would prefer to keep some cows and sell milk. But she does not have money to buy a cow.

After getting up, and worshipping the deity, she cleans the utensils from the evening before, attends 'the call of nature' which means to walk into the bushland behind the settlement. Then she brushes her teeth and takes a bath with the water that she has fetched from the well near her house. There are several wells in the settlement, one can always meet other women there and exchange the news of the day. After all this she prepares the food for the family. She wakes up the children and helps them to get ready. She feeds her husband, then her children and, last, herself.

Whenever there is day-labour, she accompanies her husband to the workplace. They take the bus into town and often have to walk a long distance to get to the building site. She works until five in the afternoon, returns home, looks after the children, cooks food. If she has no day-labour, she does housework for about three to four hours a day. When the housework is done she takes rest and chats with her neighbours.

*****

The following are extracts from my research diary; it was my first visit to Santilata after I had read the information wich another woman, who lives in the same settlement, had collected from her:

> Santilata's mud-hut is very clean, some family photos hang on one wall, the main room has a few pieces of furniture, one wooden bed, one shelf, one chair. There is another small room which serves as kitchen and storeroom. Her three little girls were with her. Santilata was somewhat overwhelmed with the joy of receiving visitors. She is very shy, soft and friendly.
>
> "When you told your story to Shanti you said that you sometimes work as a day-labourer. How does one get such work?"
>
> "Most of the times the men in the community who work as day-labourers tell the women when there are jobs. But we also go ourselves and search for work."
>
> "How much money per day do you earn if you have work?"
>
> "Twenty five rupees per day."
>
> "That is more than most women earn."
>
> "That is what my husband gets. I get twenty rupees a day, sometimes less. From that I have to spend three rupees for the bus."
>
> "Is that money paid to you or to your husband?"
>
> "To me."
>
> "What kind of work do you do?"
>
> "Carrying sand, bricks, all that."
>
> "You have this little baby. What do you do with her when you go for work?"
>
> "Now I don't go out, there is nobody to look after the baby."
>
> .....
>
> "You said that you would you like to keep cows and sell milk. Why?"
>
> "I can do anything..."
>
> "Do you mean you can sew, can make papad and so on...?"
>
> "No, I cannot do those things, but I am willing to do anything. But it is easier to be at home because of the children, and I could keep a cow at home."
>
> "Have you had cows before, or have your parents had cows?"
>
> "I do not know anything about cows."
>
> "Do you have any idea how much one cow costs, say a young cow?"
>
> "I don't know." (nor did I)

"Where would you keep the cow?"
"In the yard here in front of the house"
(The yard is a tiny patch of front garden)
"How would you feed the cow?"
(She shrugs her shoulders and smiles shyly) "I don't know."
"Where would you sell the milk?"
"To tea-stalls here in the settlement, and other shops."

.....

"Tell me about your skills; what other skills do you have?"
"Nothing."
"If you were given the chance to learn a new skill, what would you choose?"
"I would like to learn how to make pickles, papad, paper bags, all that."
"Why that?"
"Because I would not have to go to Bhubaneswar, I could do it here."
"If someone in your neighbourhood here would start such a business and would offer you employment, would you take it?"
"Yes I would. But here nobody gives employment."

.....

"Do you save money?"
"No. I used to save a bit before but I spent it all."
"Do you sometimes dream about something you would like to do or to have?"
"No, never."
"You never dream?"
"Well, I have day-dreams, sometimes."
"Do you mind if I ask you what your day-dreams are about?"
"This and that, nothing particular."

.....

After this visit we met several times, mostly together with other women of the community. Many of these other women's lives were very similar to that of Santilata: need for income, husband day-labourer, small children, no skills. The idea of setting up a savings and credit group was picked up with great enthusiasm. When I asked Santilata again about her wish to keep a cow she told me that it was not a serious wish; when Mrs.S. had interviewed her the first time the question had come as a surprise and as she felt she ought to say something, she mentioned keeping a cow because this was something that seemed easy.

After an interval of six months I visited Santilata again; she was still staying at home, looking after her children. She joined one of the new women's savings group that had been initiated during my first research period. But she has not taken up any of the ideas we had discussed during our various group meetings. If times get very bad I can still go out and do day-labour, she said.

What influences the positive-uncertain woman ?

I have met women like Santilata everywhere I have been. This type of woman is not totally negative about self-employment, but she is not sure whether she can do it, or how to do it. She is likely to say things like "I would like to do something but I don't know what" or "I would like to do this or that but...." or "Tell me what to do". What is most important is that even if she expresses a keen wish to becoming self-employed, she does not make any attempt to undertake steps towards turning her wish into a practical experience.

The indecisiveness about self-employment, the dream of "being my own boss" or earning "my own money" may accompany this woman throughout her life. She is, to some extent, not under pressure to do something about it, as there is someone in her family who earns an income and provides, however little. Or, especially if she lives on her own, she is earning some income, through casual wage-work or part-time employment; or she gets support from her family, friends or the state. She finds the idea of starting an enterprise, becoming her own boss and earning more money very desirable, but not -yet- feasible.

Helen D. typifies the English woman whose perception is influenced by factors such as the ones mentioned above:

> Helen is a single parent; before her son was born she decided not to marry the father, as she could foresee too many problems. She moved in with her widowed mother, who lived in a council house in a small village in the south of England. It was the best solution at the time, but it turned out to be a bad one; the mother was getting too old to look after the growing up boy full-time, Helen was therefore not able to work full-time and had to take on badly paid cleaning jobs in the village, as there is no regular public

transport to nearby towns or cities and she did not have the money to take driving lessons and buy a car. She began to consider the idea of becoming self-employed. She does not have any degree nor has she had any vocational training; but she knows how to arrange flowers; she also likes cooking - but her kitchen is tiny, catering would be difficult; a cleaning business would also not be a bad idea - but she is not mobile. Helen had many ideas .... Then the mother died and Helen could have moved to a more accessible place. But she feels secure in the village, she knows everybody and her son, who is now twelve years old, has his friends here and does not want to live anywhere else. Helen is always short of money and still plans to set up a business - but which one?

The uncertain woman stays at home, at least part-time, because she has children and child-care facilities are not available to her or not considered to be proper. Her positive perception of enterprise is related to her wish to stay at home with her children, but at the same time to earn money either to supplement the family income or to be more independent. It may be, that her family - parents or husbands - are against her working outside the home, or that society's norms do not allow her to work outside the house.

This type of woman usually has at least domestic skills (that is those skills required to run a family and a household).[12] She may also have, what I would call 'vernacular skills', that is skills related to the activities of her community or clan: agricultural skills, special crafts or handicrafts.[13] But she does not realise that these skills can produce cash income. And so she is keen to learn new skills: "Teach me something", "I would like to learn something" are phrases I have heard many times from women of this type of woman.

Unlike the despondent woman, the uncertain woman often belongs to a women's group, but she is one of the passive members. Sometimes the wish to be self-employed is started by a process of change that has been initiated by a women's group or by a development intervention.

The following examples shows that qualitative research - which is always a type of intervention into peoples lives, as it confronts them with new or different issues across a period of time - can set off such process of change:

Urmila D. is a widow with two daughters; they live together with Urmila's mother, her four brothers and their families in one house; five families altogether. The brothers are involved in small business activities. Urmila is not really wanted here, in India a woman belongs to her husband's family, so she should have stayed with her brother-in-law when her husband died.

She wanted to be with her mother, but now very often she feels depressed and under pressure from her brothers to leave. She would like to earn some money of her own and be independent, but did not know what to do. When I first met her, we talked about self-employment; she and her daughters make beautiful embroidery - a 'vernacular' skill - and she also proved to be an excellent cook. But she had never thought about self-employment before, had never perceived it as something feasible or even desirable for herself. The idea began to go around in her head and when I visited her again, she wanted to know many details about setting up a business, and was willing to sell to me - and not just give, as she had done before - some of her products.

The positive perception of enterprise that this woman has, is linked to the fact that regular employment is not available, or not accessible to her; or it is not suitable, because of her female gender or because she belongs to a certain caste or class. The woman who is generating income has casual, dreary, and badly paid jobs, like Helen. She may also be a seasonal worker, like Yanjuke :

Yanjuke T., a young Gambian woman, works as a chamber maid in a large hotel in Banjul, the Capital city. Each year during the off-season, for six months from April to September, the hotel closes one large wing and many of the staff are sent home. Yanjuke is one of them. She has been to school for two years "many years ago", and she started working as a chamber maid some five years ago. "I am the only one who earns money in my family", she told me. Her mother is ill, her elder sister, who lives in her mother's house, has two small children to look after and cannot go out for work. Yanjuke's father has two other wives with families (The Gambia's population is mainly Muslim, with extensive polygamy), he does not give money to Yanjuke's mother "but sometimes he brings gifts". There is a grandmother who lives in a village outside Banjul and who gives them vegetables and other food from time to time.

In the off-season "I sit at home because I cannot find another job". Does she have savings from the months before? The hotel gives her an extra month's wage as a sort of compensation for being laid off, but that does not take her far, wages are very low; often it is used to pay off debts. Why does she not engage in some micro-enterprise activities like other women? There are so many women in the tourist markets selling tie-and-dye articles or batiks. But Yanjuke does not have the skills and, in the first place, she is skeptical about the income that she could make from producing garments. "The women at the tourist market complain that they don't sell very much", she says. "Don't you have any other skills that could help you to earn money?" I asked her. "No", she said, "nothing; I would like to learn something; tell me what to do."

The uncertain woman neither has the formal skills nor the right contacts to get regular employment; she lives in an environment where employment opportunities are very limited anyhow. But - and this is very important - if regular employment was easily available, she would prefer to be employed rather than being self-employed. She wants to be told what to do.

References and Notes

[1]   Prostitution: It may be that some women go into prostitution for reasons of "higher profitability", or for the sake of "adventure", or hoping for a more glamorous life; these are more likely to be women from middle-class backgrounds. To assume that utterly poor women are pulled into this "enterprise" by similar considerations is cynical. Begging: There are some who say that begging is a micro-enterprise activity; that many people beg because they have made an informed decision, so to say, about income prospects. I can merely hope that people of such view may get the chance to go begging.

[2]   Bernstein et al, 1992, pages 13-26

[3]   ibid.

[4]   Chambers et.al, 1989, p.10

[5]   see in Bernstein et.al., 1992, p. 22

[6]   see Amis, 1994, p.635

[7]   this title of a book by Erich Fromm, 1984, refers to mankind's fear of individual freedom; Fromm describes how the sense of isolation may drive people to a submission to an all-powerful state and does nowhere refer to "fear of freedom" as a "gender issue", that is something that may be stronger in women than in men or vice-versa; yet when I first read this book it immediately also brought up images of women

[8]   see Dowling, 1994, p. 30 and later

[9]   One of the most interesing because non-conformist and creative books on this subject is Ivan Illich"s "Gender",1983; the Open University has produced a series of very good texts which I would like to recommend to any "beginner" in this subject: Knowing Women, Defining Women, Inventing Women and Imagining Women (see bibliography)

[10] referred to in "Why can"t a woman be more like a man?", Oxford Today, Vol 8, No.1, p.24-27

[11] I would like to remind the reader at this point that I did not research personal, that is psychological characteristics, but some were so obvious and a matter of mere common sense understanding; also, I agree with Fromm, 1984, that the basic entity of the social process is the individual and that "to understand the dynamics of the social process we must understand the dynamics of the psychological processes operating within the individual, just as to understand the individual we must see him in the context of the culture which moulds him".

[12] For statistic purposes in India, for example, domestic or household activities are divided between "conventional domestic activities" and "expanded domestic activities"; the latter includes activities such as free collection of goods, that is vegetables, roots, firewood, fish, cowdung, cattle feed), maintenance of kitchen gardens, orchards etc., work in poultry or dairy, sewing, tailoring, weaving etc. for household use, water collection and tutoring of children. This impressive list implies that most "housewives" have a large range of "domestic skills".

[13] "Vernacular" in its original Latin use means those things that are homemade, homespun, homegrown, not made for the market but for home use only (see Illich, 1983, p.68) I use this term for those skills which a woman has learned during childhood or adolescence from her parents or others in the community and which are related to traditional (in India often caste-specific) occupations.

3 "In times of need women get busy":[1] The enterprising women

What do they do, the enterprising women?

Several times I have been asked to carry out 'training needs assessment' studies among women involved in enterprise in various countries. The official visiting schedules of such studies have mostly taken me to women who had just started a formal enterprise, or where already quite successfully involved in such enterprise. But I have learned more about the needs of 'enterprising women' when informally visiting market places such as the following:

Brikama, The Gambia, a market place: Four women are seated in a row, two of them selling soft drinks in small plastic bags, the other two selling pancakes. All four spend the whole day just outside the market, in front of a row of market stalls along the dust-road, waiting for customers. They cannot afford to pay the fee for a proper stall. The pancakes are displayed on two large plates, placed on low stools right by the road, half covered with old, filthy plastic sheets, a half-hearted and unsuccessful attempt to keep flies and dust out. The soft drinks are sold out of small cooling boxes, of the kind that people use for picnics. The variety is displayed on top of the boxes: sad little plastic bags filled with liquid of dubious colours and three different, artificial tastes.

All four women complain about the small quantities they are able to sell. The soft-drinks sellers think it is because of the 'cool' season (it was around 28 degrees Celsius) that people did not want so many soft drinks these days. But they do not know what else to produce, so they will just go on doing this, they say.

The 'pancake women' had started this kind of business, because at one time it had seemed to be a good idea, and other women had been quite successful. Now there is very little demand, yet they do not know what else to produce. It did not occur to them, that lack of demand might be related to low quality and hygiene of their products. So they just prepare a small quantity every day, hoping to sell it all. We ask why they do not share duties, instead of all four sitting in front of the market the whole day.

Their answer: The quantities produced each day are so small, that it would not work. We have heard similar answers before. Is it not rather because there is a lot of mistrust among these women?, my Gambian colleague and I are wondering. The four of them are involved in this business to keep their families going, but none of them has any concept of 'business'. Money is used for private purposes as it comes in; product leftovers are not sold at lower prices, but given away to family and friends at the end of the day.

None of the women has received any assistance or training; they thought there must be people out there who could give them advice. But they do not know where to find such people. Nobody ever talked to them about these things, nobody had ever addressed the kind of problems we were discussing now. They feel that talking to us is already helping them, as they had never thought about things like hygiene or selling leftovers at lower prices or maybe even consider to learn a new skill.

But then one of the four women, the one who has been quiet so far, says: "One can not do anything about good or bad business; everything depends on luck; God is responsible for what you have or don't have".

These and others I will be presenting in this chapter - some of them more successful than the four women above - are the women the Wall Street Journal article, that I mentioned in Chapter One, referred to. They are the poor women on whose income generating activities so much expectations are thrust in so many anti-poverty programmes. The four women's activities show many typical characteristics: the women's business is informal, using local resources and traditional, mostly 'domestic' skills; they often work from home, combining income generation with household duties; very few can read and write, and most have never received any formal training; their market is the immediate neighbourhood, with mainly poor people, earning them a very low income. Yet without these women's income, their children would probably not go to school, nor in many cases have sufficient food and shelter.

Women like these have been and are the subject of many books and articles. I shall therefore not go into the details and constraints of their business dealings, but only give a brief summary of the main characteristics of these women's micro-enterprise activities:

- *Most of their business activities can be found in the traditional parts of the manufacturing and service sectors; they run low return enterprises on the margin of economic viability:*

In manufacturing women are mostly involved in food processing of the kind that I have described at the beginning of this chapter; in making women's and children's clothing; and in handicrafts.

In the service sector, women are mainly to be found in domestic services like cleaning, washing and cooking; some of these services are provided in form of wage labour, others are carried out at home (washing, cooking/catering).

Trade is another important source of employment and enterprise for women. In rural areas, women subsistence farmers are often also petty or part-time traders involved in retailing processed and raw food, and other essential goods.

In urban areas, illiterate and unskilled women are often involved in similar petty activities, and they operate from their homes. Very few women here are involved in retail and wholesale of farm products, and only literate women seem to trade in modern type goods like clothing, cosmetics and jewellery.

- *Most women's enterprises are micro-enterprises*, that is employing only up to nine people (ILO[2] definition of micro-enterprise). According to UNIFEM,[3] an estimated seventy per cent of micro-enterprises world-wide are run by women.

  Some researchers have found, that women are not as interested in business growth as are men: they seem to have little time or inclination to take on the management and other hussles associated with larger enterprises.

- *Their micro-enterprises are mostly operating in the 'informal' sector of the economy*, without licenses and registration, taxation; this has advantages but also threats.

- *Their enterprises own very meagre capital and assets.* Men can avail of household resources, sometimes even resources from their wives' enterprise activities; they also have somewhat easier access to institutional credit; and they can dedicate more time to their enterprises, as they do not have the responsibilities of day-to-day reproductive work (that is work which is not considered to be 'productive' as it does not generate income: cooking, cleaning, rearing children, caring for elderly parents, growing vegetables for home consumption etc.; according to a UN statistic women do 90 per cent of this type of work). Women can only avail of very small amounts of money, often saved from the food budget. There are various reasons for women's limited access to capital:

- more than men women lack the common forms of collateral required for credit like for example land title, a house, cattle, co-operative membership;
- in some countries women cannot get credit without the consent of their husbands or other male family members;
- the loans they need are often too small and therefore too unprofitable for banking and financing institutions;
- omen are less confident, and sometimes hesitant, to approach formal financial institutions where they usually will have to do transactions with male staff.

Most of these enterprises involve traditional, labour intensive skills: *women's enterprises rely on much more rudimentary technology than men.* Various studies show how men take over when a new technology is introduced, or when their wives enterprises start growing.

Women's enterprises are often home-based, and women have therefore been called "invisible women entrepreneurs"[4] or "invisible hands".[5] Women working from home are also often called 'home-based workers'; most home-based workers anywhere are women, in so-called developing and developed countries, and there is an increasing number of associations or networks of such home-based workers in many countries.[6] There are two types of home-based workers: the 'piece-rate workers' and the 'own account-workers'.[7] The piece-rate workers get their raw materials from a contractor or employer and deliver the finished goods to the same person or firm; sometimes contractors loan the equipment to their piece-rate workers, others don't and the women have to get or use their own. The difference between these women and women employees is, that the former do not get the benefits that usually come with employment, like sick leave, or regularity of payment, or a certain degree of job security.

Own account workers usually buy their own raw material, process it at home and sell the finished goods themselves, either directly to end-consumers or to retailers or wholesalers. There are various consequences of working from home: less access to customers, to innovations and price information, dependence on verbal transaction with few people. Working at home most often means using the kitchen or another family room, sometimes the only room, for production. It often means that the women have to clear everything away when husbands or other family members come home.

- *They rely more than men on family labour* (children, other family members). This also perpetuates forms of child-labour and especially disadvantages girl-children: a mother will more easily involve her daughter in her activities, while a son is send to school where possible; in most societies schooling for girls is not seen as important as schooling for boys.

- *They diversify their enterprise activities rather than specialise*; this is due to various reasons:
  - thin and fragmented markets in rural areas limit the quantity of any single product a woman is able to sell
  - different activities at various times of the year for survival (woman may be engaged in agricultural day labour during the agricultural season(s), process and sell certain types of food during another season, and weave and sell baskets occasionally)
  - investing small amounts of money in various activities may be less risky than investing everything in one business.

Another important reason is the unstable economy of their countries; this means that women are wise to spread their risks. An example is Zambia, a country with political and economic instability; high inflation, corruption, lawlessness makes it difficult for any business to succeed and remain stable. Some years ago my husband and I together with colleagues of a Zambian training institution conducted a short business training programme for some twenty women. The women were mostly from lower income groups and had been or still were working as employees (secretaries, catering officers) in Government offices or small businesses, or as school teachers. When we met them again a year later, many of these women had kept their jobs while running their enterprise or enterprises.

The above list of characteristics of women's micro-enterprises seems to make up a recipe for economic failure. Yet such a view neglects the important social functions that these micro-enterprises have. Louise Dignard and Jose Havet[8] have rightly criticised the "non-traditional work syndrome" - that is the attempts to get women away from these low-return, traditional activities - that can be noticed in micro-and small enterprise programmes for women and in the literature. One of the problems of such this is that it implies

> "...that women should 'conquer' some of men's domains of activities and they embark on this quest on an equal footing with men, as independent individuals. In this view, greater gender equality becomes homogenization of gender roles, resulting from a one-sided change: women's roles become more like men's, but men's roles do not evolve." [9]

Women lives are far more than men's embedded in a web of social relationship and responsibilities. Enterprising women run enterprises, families, homes, even local social services; enterprising men run enterprises.

Below I present three types of enterprising women: the negative-pragmatic, the positive-pragmatic and the ambitious. Most women can be called pragmatic; it means to be realistic and concerned with practical results. The negative-pragmatic women don't believe that enterprise is a feasible or attractive solution to their problems, but they are never-the-less 'enterprising' in the sense of the word as I have introduced it in Chapter One: they are lucky enough to have found some sort of wage work.

The borderline between the two other types is diffuse, for the reasons explained in Chapter One: they are self-employed by force (they are pragmatic) or by choice (they are ambitious). I believe, that the main difference between them is the quality of their skills (which includes skills in communicating, and which are heavily influenced by their socio-economic background, the chances the women had to learn anything) and of their experience, the time spent in the enterprise they are running.

"A bird in the hand is better than two in the bush": The negative-pragmatic woman

A few women among those I met, seem to be pragmatic, but their pragmatism has a negative quality, a negative view of 'enterprise'.

These women are lucky enough to have found wage work as cleaners, house-helpers or day-labourers, and they do not want to generate income in any other way, although the work is badly paid. They are very realistic about their possibilities and their attitude goes with the proverb "a bird in the hand is worth two in the bush". They do not believe that they can start any enterprise which would give them the same kind of income.

From an enterprise perspective one could say, that most employed women have a negative-pragmatic perception of self-employment, because although many of them complain about low pay, bad working conditions and inflexible working hours, most women do not see self-employment as a feasible or desirable alternative to employment.

Kuri, the woman I introduce below as a typical case, is an extreme case on the borderline of 'despondency'. But in some way she is typical, because throughout our meetings she was consistent in her negative view of any other type of self-employment or enterprise; she knew that she lacked the skills, and the resources, to do anything else but cleaning other people's houses.

"In this work I have practice": The story of Kuri B.

Kuri lives in Berhampur, a large commercial town about 180 km south-west of Orissa's capital Bhubaneswar. It is the centre of the famous Berhampur silk weaving and some 210,000 people live here. The part of Berhampur where Kuri lives with her children is part of the old city. The streets here are very narrow and lined with rows of old, one to two story buildings. Small, open waste-water drains run along many streets. Many houses used to be lived in by wealthier people, who have left this community, renting their houses out. Often two or three families occupy now what used to be a one-family house. Many small business people live here, shop-keepers, traders; traditional, mainly home-based activities are, for example, the manufacture of papads (or papadums), leaf-plates, paper-bags or sweets. Very often these activities are family activities, with specific tasks for men and for women. Often husband and wife run such a 'production unit' together and if business is good, they employ girls and women from the neighbourhood. On the fringes of this community one finds rows of poorer, smaller houses, some so fragile that it seems they are only holding together because they can lean on their neighbours. Kuri lives in one of them.

Here is Kuri's story:

My life is full of hardships and I have no peace. My mother died when I was an infant. Father did not bother about us; he knew only to fight with us, beat us that we may hand over to him the few coins we earned by our labour. His obsession was drink. Only grandmother, father's mother, looked after us. She was our refuge to hide from his harassment.

From early childhood I and my sister joined grandmother in thrashing paddy, pounding rice, frying puffed rice, all that. We also worked as labourers in the season of transplanting and harvesting paddy. But all this agricultural work lasted only fifty to sixty days a year. I am a fisher-woman by caste. But from generations we never went fishing.

Grandmother was anxious to get us married, lest she died before we were settled. My father said it was not his concern to get us married. I had not yet reached puberty, then. From Ampua I came to Berhampur after marriage.

My husband and myself used to be put in one room for the night. He used to pull me, drag me and I used to be scared and cry. I also tried pulling the latch and running out. After some months I suddenly got periods. My next experience was that of feeling very hungry early morning. Not being able to resist hunger, I used to escape into my aunt's house and ask her for food to satisfy my hunger, since my family members never believed me and ignored my need. After a few months my stomach bulged out. Neighbours said "Look at her, the other day she was a child, now she herself carries one".

I am the mother of five children and my eldest child is Laxmi. I was in my grandmother's house when I was about to deliver her. I was suffering intensely. Seeing my agony, the neighbours told my grandmother to take me to the hospital. So she brought me to City Hospital, covering a distance of seven km by cycle rickshaw. As I climbed the steps of the hospital, suddenly the baby fell down. However the hospital personnel did the needful and both of us, baby and myself, were safe. After three months of the birth of my last child I underwent family planning surgery in the same hospital.

My husband was a drunkard. He ill-treated me, insulted me, beat me. Very rarely did he give me five or three Rupees for the family expense. Often I sat with my little children in the dark, because we had no kerosene to light a lamp. I did request neighbours and relatives for some help as I could not go anywhere leaving the children. Many times I slept off hungry feeding the children with morsels given by others.

From the last ten years I work in various houses doing all the housework. My Laxmi and myself form a good pair and we work in collaboration. I worked in Mr.Roi's house and Mr. Patra's house for five years. They paid 50 and 45 Rupees respectively in a month. Gradually, Mr. Roi's family members began to blame me unnecessarily though I worked very hard washing utensils, clothes and sweeping and scrubbing the floor. I stopped working in that house. One day since there was heavy rain my daughter and myself did not appear at Mr. Patra's house. The next day he quipped satirically what the mother and the daughter must have been doing staying at home the whole day. I felt very insulted and we stopped going there. Many times whenever I am really hungry and request that any left over food be given to me the family members keep on muttering "Nothing is there, everything is over yesterday itself", and so on. I feel very angry to hear such make-believe stories. Only a few families occasionally share a little food with me.

The house we live in is our ancestral house. Every day I rise before dawn and complete my personal needs and take bath at the water pipe on the roadside. There I wash utensils and fetch some water for the house. On Monday mornings I go to the temple with a little ghee, plantain and so, which I buy the previous evening. When I get up I call my Laxmi to rise. But she rises in her own time and completes her personal things and goes to the families to work.

Till a few years ago, we used firewood for cooking. As firewood is very costly, we use kerosene stove now, bringing kerosene from the ration shop. In some months we get two to three kilograms of rice from the ration shop. Mostly we purchase it from the grocery shop. We never prepare tea or coffee. A few times when I am sick and if Laxmi forces me I buy a cup of tea from the nearby tea-shop for 50 or 60 paise [one rupee = hundred paise] and both of us share it.

My husband's end came most unexpectedly. For about ten days he kept on saying that he was not feeling well. I took him to Dr. Das and we bought the medicine. But in a few days his speech stopped. I was worried. I bought some milk for 25 paise and a few slices of bread and fed him, but his condition worsened. I took him to City Hospital. I had to borrow 200 Rupees to buy four bottles of saline. With the fear that he might fall off the cot I used to rest a while on the edge of his cot in the night when I too longed for a bit of sleep. Nurses scolded me saying whether I was the patient or what. So one night, when I was asleep on the ground close to his cot, all of a sudden he fell from the cot. Blood flowed from his forehead. I did not know what to do.

Somehow I called the doctor and they put some stitches on this forehead holding a torch light. Within a few hours he died.

My Laxmi's marriage is another bolt from the blue. Laxmi was promised in marriage to a relative of ours; but by the time she grew up he was already married to another woman. In spite of that my sister-in-law and myself decided to get Laxmi married to this man. After marriage he stayed in our house for fifteen days. His previous wife, who was already pregnant, came and waited on our veranda for a number of hours. They thought there was some witchcraft involved which makes him stay in our house. This lady shouted, screamed, fought and dragged her man out of our house. We, too, resigned ourselves saying that we do not need him.

I had a lot of desire that my children should become educated. I took Laxmi to school. I spanked her hard to stay in school. But she simply cried and refused to go to school. Had she listened to me, her condition would not be as it is now.

My second child is Devi. He attended school for a year. Then he began working in a cycle shop. A neighbouring widow enticed him a year ago. That woman used to fall on the young boys when they sat on her veranda, chatting among themselves. Once a neighbour brought the news that she was having an affair with my son in broad day light. I rushed there with my daughter. Hearing me, Devi went out through the back door. I was so angry that I stripped the woman naked. She stood there mute and speechless. She is willing to give me anything from her house, but who wants her things when she misbehaves so shamelessly with my son. Now my son has left for Bombay. He sent me a letter. He is working there in a cycle market.

My third child is Pradeep. He works in a hotel, washing glasses and cleaning tables. Since my other children did not go to school, I did not attempt to send him to school. He gets two Rupees and fifty paise per day. He gives me the two Rupees and he spends the rest for himself.

My forth child is Shanti. She had two years of schooling. Then I sent her to look after my niece's child. Shanti stays in her house and she provides her the necessities. By supplying water to three families, Shanti earns an additional 60 Rupees per month which my sister-in-law keeps for her marriage.

My youngest son is Suresh. He is in standard IV in Military Line School. Nowadays at the ration shop they demand signature and not thumb impression. So I make him to sign. These days I spent forty Rupees for his books, cutting down our food expenses. For four months I had sent him for extra coaching paying ten Rupees per month. Now they expect fifteen so I can't afford to sent him. In the evening I tell him to go to his aunt's house to read as they have electricity. She is my own sister. She is better off and I am like this. My bad luck!

*****

From my research diary: About three months after she had told her story, I met Kuri again in the house of one of her employers.

"Kuri, I think you are not very happy to sit here and talk with us."
"I am so tired, I work for five families, one hour each in the morning to wash clothes, and one hour each in the evening to wash their utensils."
"That is a lot of work; how much do they pay you ?"
"In three houses I get 100 Rupees each in a month; in the other two houses I get only 60 Rupees a month. My son also gives me some money, about 10 Rupees a day. Laxmi is not working, she went to her husband's house."
"Does she come to see you ?"
"She comes now and then"
"And what about the other wife of Laxmi's husband ?"
"She has gone away. Now my elder son is trying to find work, it is difficult. The younger one has a job in a tea stall, he gives me 10 Rupees a day from his earnings."
"Have you ever thought of doing a different job, instead of cleaning other people's houses ?"
"I cannot do anything else."
"Why ?"
"In this work I have practice; I cannot go about in the sun; I will go on working in other people's houses. In my caste women make and sell muri [puffed rice]. I can't, I would not earn enough for my family."

Then she gets up and says she has to go and get guraku, a sort of drug that many people take; one has to rub it onto the gums. Many poor people take it, because it takes the feeling of hunger away and makes one feel less tired. It costs 25 paise for 25 grams; that seems to be enough for two days.

After some minutes Kuri comes back, saying that she already feels much better. She uses the drug every day, she says; it makes her feel much better.

"If someone would offer you to learn a new skill, maybe something that would earn you more money, what would you like to learn ?"

(she does not understand the question; Sister N. explains; she still does not know what to do with the question; Sister N. gives her examples of things one can learn) "I would not do , I don't want to learn I am old and tired."

"Do you sometimes dream about something you would like to like to do or to have; some wish, something special ?"

"I never dream. Nothing."

Typical features of the negative-pragmatic woman

The family of the negative pragmatic woman depends on her income, as she is the main or only income earner. She earns low but regular wages through some form of employment or self-employment, usually as a domestic helper or an unskilled day labourer working for a contractor. She does not see other forms of self-employment or enterprise as a desirable alternative.

Ulash B. is a young Indian woman of about eighteen years. She lives with her parents in a small village; their home is a tiny mud hut located on what seems a rather large piece of land in comparison to this hut. There is a little pond and the plot looks quite nice, but the hut is so low, that one has to bend down to get into the only room. Ulash's father, who has leprosy, sleeps in one corner. There is some shelter at one side of the hut for the sheep, the 'kitchen' is in the open and there is another tiny shelter, which seems to be a storage room.

Ulash's father does not work because of his illness which, so it is said, he caught from the prostitutes of the railway platform in the capital city. Ulash's mother used to work as a day labourer whenever she got work, but now, at hardly forty years of age, she feels too old and tired and so Ulash remains as the main income earner of the family, as her younger brother goes to school and the older one is a "lazy and useless scoundrel" (so other women in the village say). Ulash's main source of income is day labour, working as a farm labourer during the farming seasons and as a day labourer cutting stones. She also keeps three sheep. They cost 450 to 470

Rupees each, and she bought them with a interest-free loan, which she got from a local NGO. Once they are grown, she will sell them for about 600 to 700 Rupees. People here do not take sheep milk or cheese, so there is no income to be made from that. Ulash does not know much about sheep; if they do not eat well, they may be ill, she thought. But the next veterinary service is far from here and although officially a free service is provided, one has to bribe them to come. Ulash has no ambition to start a 'sheep farm' or some such; as the only income earner of the family she needs a regular income, however miserable it may be.

Whatever kind of enterprise activities are happening around the negative-pragmatic woman, has no important effect on her attitudes, because hers is a narrow view of the world, narrowed by day-to-day worries for the family. Other women in her community are earning income through other forms of self-employment, but even if these incomes are better, the negative-pragmatic woman does not see other women as role models.

B. Parmer is the leader of the children's food unit of a co-operative in Ahmedabad, India; she is twenty two years old, has intermediate school education and was trained by a large women's organisation in Mumbai for two weeks in 'food-processing' to do this job. She earns 25 Rupees per day here; her husband left her and she is earning her keep. When I asked about her future plans she said that she would like to remain in the co-operative and do more or less the same; she has not thought about anything different although she would like to be better off. Could she imagine working for herself, setting up her own business one day, like other women in this city have done? No, she said, she preferred the group support, she could not imagine being on her own.

The negative-pragmatic woman is likely to be a widow or abandoned woman, who has found wage work which is very badly paid but fairly stable, and the payment is regular. She is the sole or main income earner and is completely dependent on that income, which she does not want to put at risk or give up. And if there is an extended family network at all, its members are too poor to give much support. She is landless and lives in an environment, where women can sometimes find regular, non-seasonal employment or wage-work.

The negative-pragmatic woman does not have time to spare, because she works full-time; apart from earning money, she also has to look after her family. This lack of time influences her negative inclination in two ways: she does not have time to look for alternatives, and she is too tired to venture out in search of better paid jobs or enterprise.

> During an assignment looking at women's food processing enterprises in Gujarat, India, I met seven women running a 'tea canteen' for a Government department. The women work here in an tiny shed next to the office building. They don't have enough space and make only tea and coffee which is served in the offices. The group leader received a short training in food processing from a women's organisation in Mumbai.
>
> The women rotate, they work in another unit of the co-operative after three months, because otherwise they would have to be employed permanently.
>
> None of the women does any food-processing at home; the group leader said, that in fact she had never done anything else but this work here. Her day starts at 7.30 a.m. and she gets home by 8 p.m., so she does not have time to think about any other activity that could earn a better income. All of them would have liked to earn more money, but there are very few employment opportunities of a 'decent' kind and they are all members of the co-operative, which has some advantages; they feel safer here than in other employment, they said.

Apart from domestic skills, the negative-pragmatic woman may have other 'vernacular' skills, which she may use in her work. Other women in her community may use such skills to earn a slightly better income with less humiliation, but this has not increased her desire to run any such enterprise, as she does not believe, that she has the means to turn her skills into a business.

> I met Mary C. when in Jamaica; she was a domestic helper working for several of my colleagues. Mary had done this work for many years, working for three to four families at a time. She had four children of two husbands, both having disappeared soon after the birth of the second child, or so she said. She was complaining about the low pay she was receiving from her employers for doing "all the dirty work". "Why", I asked her, "don't you save some money and set up your own business, like so many other women here?" "No", she said, " what would I do? Now I know at least what amount of cash I am taking home at the end of the week; those women don't!"

The negative-pragmatic woman may belong to a women's group, for example a savings group, but she usually does not have enough time and

energy to spend much time with her peers. Her energy goes into her work -
outside and at home. Her most important 'network' is her employers, that is
people who - if need be - can refer her to others who may be able to offer
similar jobs.

She does not respond positively to any suggestions from outside to
change her life; she does not want change - may even be frightened of change
- because she cannot perceive, that something more positive could happen to
her; she is too busy and accepts, or rather puts up with, her present condition.

"Getting down to business"[10]: The positive-pragmatic woman

These are the women who just get on with their enterprise activity. They
generate self-employed income, alone or in a group, but they do it, because
they need money and have no other source; they would take a job or start
anything different, if that would bring more money.

A crop, a shop, a job: The story of Kasai J.

Kasai is a tribal woman from Koraput, the southernmost district of Orissa on
the border to the State of Andrah Pradesh. Like all Indian districts, Koraput
is divided into 'Blocks', each comprising a town and/or several villages. The
capital of the block in which Kasai lives, is a small town with a population
of approximately 10,000 people, and with one hundred odd villages under its
government. The scattered villages are very isolated; public transport only
services the villages and towns along the few tarmac roads and from some
places villagers have to walk hours to get to the nearest roadside or village
market.

The majority of the population are tribal people, who mainly live in the
small, scattered villages in the hilly areas. Very few villages have electricity,
but when they do, it is mostly used for lighting the village square; very rarely
do villagers have electricity in their houses. Some of the villages in the block
do not even have a well; the villagers get their water from a nearby river.
Schools, hospitals, banks are to be found only in the larger towns, and even
health posts for some villages are within a day or more of walking distance.
Fuel for cooking, that is fire wood and sometimes cow dung, is collected
mainly by the women and children; some villages have gobar- or bio-gas

plants, using animal and plant waste to produce fuel that is mainly used for cooking.

Apart from agriculture the main employer of the area, although not for the tribal women, is NALCO, the National Aluminium Corporation, with huge bauxite mines and a complete small town built for its employees and managers. Because of these mines many tribal people have been re-settled; but although they received compensation in the form of houses and money, and a number of them were employed by NALCO, it has caused and still is causing great anger and distress among them because not only did many of them lose their land and their homes but also much of the forest with its 'minor forest products' like roots, leaves, herbal plants and fruits, which to them was an important source for subsistence and cash income.

Landless families or those with too little land to generate surplus, earn at least part of their livelihood from working as day-labourers (coolies) on the agricultural land of tribal or non-tribal land-owners or for sub-contractors in road construction and maintenance, or in timber cutting. One important source of income is liquor. The brewing is mainly done by non-tribal people, but the liquor is often sold by tribal people - to tribal people; their menfolk - and often women - are the best customers. With alcohol come the many problems: violence in the family, loss of income or savings, even loss of land. Almost all the women I have met in Koraput talked about these problems, but some women still earn the main part of their cash income by selling liquor.

Kasai J. never sold liquor, but she might have done so. This is her story:

"I am now forty years old. When I was small, my father died and my mother deserted me, to marry another man and go away. My maternal uncle took pity on me and took me to his house. He kept me at his home, so as to marry me to his son. While I was small, I did not learn how to read and write. In fact, I was scared of the teacher. When I was small, I used to go to the forest as well as do contract labour work and then give my earnings to my uncle. A few days passed like this, when I was a bit older, my uncle married me off to his son. A few months after marriage I gave birth to a son and then a daughter. After a few days, my husband died. While he was alive, he used to drink liquor and always used to hit me. After my husband died, my problem increased again. After he died, I had even thought of going away with another man, only because of my two children I did not go. I used to work as a labourer, in order to keep my children alive. My in-laws said "our son is dead, so why are you here". But because my children were small, I had to stay with them.

Ten years ago there was a lot of problem for food, clothing and money in general. If we did labourer work, the men used to get four Rupees for a day's work, and the women got three Rupees. With that money, it used to be very difficult to manage. If anybody would come to visit our village, we used to be very scared. We used to depend on the contractor to get us labourers' work in the village. If needed, we used to take loans from the contractor or money-lender and pay high interest. Whatever farming we did, we used to sell our produce to the money-lender and get a bit of money. If needed, I mortgaged my land, house and jewellery, with the moneylender. If we were sick, we used to call the witch doctor in order to cure us - providing them with chicken, liquor and so on.

We did not know what studying was, and we were scared to send our children to school. We used to consider the rich money-lender and the government officials to be our god. If there was some problem in the village, the menfolk would set up a panchayat [village council] meeting. When the men did not allow the womenfolk to sit in the village meetings, we had to obey that also. Men spent the hard-earned money on liquor and then hit the womenfolk - even then we did not have the strength to do anything about this. For every problem that we had, we never used to sit together to discuss and try and solve it. Whosoever had the problem, it was their headache. We used to pray to the gods when we had difficulties - we used to think that when the gods were angry with us, then we had to suffer pain and sorrow. In our village, people sold farm produce, did labourer work, and sold leaves from the forest, in order to survive. Whatever I used to earn earlier by working as a labourer, it was hardly enough for dal [lentils], salt, chillies and saag [spinach]. We sometimes did not get labourer's work in the village. In order to work as a labourer we used to go to different villages and work very hard. Even then the contractors will not pay us more than three Rupees.

Now everybody in our village is slowly realising, that because we do not study, the moneylenders and contractors are able to cheat us. Now after knowing everything, we are trying to study ourselves and also educate our children. By not being united earlier, we used to face many problems; to solve that, we have now all got together to form an union sort of thing. Now if there is difficulty, we call a village meeting and think of solving that problem.

Earlier, whatever the rich people said was right - we used to obey and listen to them. Now we think ourselves about what is right and what would be convenient to us. When we used to get loans from moneylenders, we had to pay sixty Rupees as interest on every hundred Rupees that we took as loan. So we have formed a sort of bank, from where we take loans and use when needed. By this, we have stopped taking loans from the moneylender. We also opened a night school in the village. In order to do better farming, we tried by ourselves to come up with different methods and farm the crops which would give us more money.

In the past our people used to survive on the leaves, fruits and vegetables of the forest. Now that we do not have a forest, we are in trouble. But we have got together to make our own orchards; we have planted mangoes, jack fruits, guavas, pomegranates, lemon trees.

Over two years ago I learned carpentry work. After learning this and after having been educated, I am able to take part in the village meetings and speak for myself. By farming tuti koli [cashew] on my land, I am earning more money. This tuti koli farming is done three times a year. If I sell this raw, I get sixty five Rupees per kilogram. By selling this raw, with whatever money we get we buy salt, chillies and clothes. Because of my education and higher earnings, I feel as if I have developed a much greater strength than what I had earlier. Whatever squabbles we had in our house earlier, that is no longer there. Whatever we speak in the village, the villagers do listen to us women. Earlier the menfolk used to work on the plough and the women used to do weeding, cooking and other housework. The men used to think that they are earning while the women are not earning, and they used to think that women are there to do the domestic work. By being able to do all this work, I feel that I have got more strength than before.

Since we now have gobar-gas [biogas] at home, we do not have to spend money on buying kerosene. We now earn about 900 Rupees in most months in our house. I myself do almost all the work. Apart from farming, I do contractor work during the seasons.

After having learnt everything in the village, I thought that if we women save our money, it will come in use some day. For that, we collect five Rupees every month from each house and keep it in the bank. If the bank people keep the money, it does not get lost. We get interest on this money. If we keep money at home, it is bound to get spent, that is why we decided to keep some money in the bank.

I myself think that in future, apart from doing carpentry work myself, I will also teach this to different people. Besides, all of us are planning to get together in the village and decide on the members for the village council. If I become a member then maybe I can help the womenfolk of the village."

During one of my earlier visits to Kasai's village I recorded the following in my diary:

"On our way to the village Mrs. P., who together with her husband runs a local NGO in this area, told me about the progress in the village; a group of women, among them Kasai J., got five acres of land from central government, they planted mulberry trees for rearing silk worms; it is a research project from the central government; but the women own the land and get all the returns.

In village J. we met Kasai ; she took us to the mulberry plantation, she was very proud and cheerful. She insisted that we should climb the fence to see the mulberry trees, she picked the ripe, sweet mulberry fruits for us, and showed us the different kinds of trees.

If all goes well, a lot of money is involved. According to Mrs. P. the women could make up to 30,000 Rupees in one harvest (four times a year). Could it be true that Kasai, the woman who walked bare-footed through the village when I first met her, is going to be a wealthy woman? Kasai herself is full of optimism - to her it seems that whatever comes it can never be as bad as it had been some ten years ago."

Five years later my husband and I went to visit the village again:

"Kasai does not look one day older and is still as cheerful as ever. She showed us her shop; it still consisted of a few goods, stored in one corner of one of her two rooms; but she is now also the proud owner of a scale, and she has electricity! And what about the sericulture project? Well, this was a longer story:

Since 1992 five women had been trained in the whole sequence of operations, from cultivating the mulberry to rearing the silk worms. The local NGO also raised the sum of 70,000 Rupees to purchase and install a cocoon reeling machine in the village, so that the women could be trained to reel the silk from their cocoons.

Twelve married women were trained by a skilled craftsman, whom the NGO brought from Andhra Pradesh. They were organised into a co-operative, and in the first year of production, they produced a quantity of good quality silk, which the craftsman took to Bangalore and sold for 40,000 Rupees. The women were happy to have the extra money. But they found the regular work very onerous. The craftsman decided, that in future it might be possible to obtain a more regular supply of cocoons from women in other villages, whom the NGO had trained to raise silk worms. They could buy the surplus mulberry leaf from the women of J., or even grow it in their own villages.

The following year the results were not so good. The women, among them Kasai, preferred to collect cashew and tamarind from their new forest, where they could work at their own pace, and as they wished. Some of them wanted to uproot the mulberry trees in their part of the five acres plot and replace them with ginger, since the NGO had identified a new high yielding variety. The income from this would not be as much as from the complete cycle of producing mulberry leaves, silk worm rearing and silk reeling, but it would involve far less work.

The women had also become more interested in cashew. During this year they earned a total of 50,000 Rupees from selling cashew, and the NGO had showed them how they could get a higher price, by storing and drying the cashews, rather than selling them straight off the trees. The women knew, that it was possible to earn far more by processing the cashews. The manual process was very slow and tedious, and required great skill, but the women had heard that there was a machine which could do the same process. They wondered whether the NGO might obtain one for them.

In the meantime, the craftsman whom the NGO had employed to introduce sericulture had another suggestion. His wife was a skilled weaver, and she wanted to establish her own family business in J. They would lease the mulberry plantation, and the reeling machine from the village co-operative, and employ the women to pick the leaves, to raise the worms and to reel the silk. Possibly, they might also train them to weave if the business went well. Kasai told us, that she and the other women would be happy to lease their land, since they disliked the responsibility of managing it. The lady's husband would continue to be employed by the NGO. He would introduce sericulture to more villages, and his wife would thus have an assured source of cocoons in case the viallge of J. could not produce enough.

Kasai has not become rich but she is doing well; she has a small income from her shop, quite a substantial income from her farming activities and she still does agricultural labourer jobs for bigger farmers in the area; her motto seems to be: it is important to keep one's options open and to spread the risk!"

Typical features of the positive-pragmatic woman

There are millions of women all over the world like Kasai and the four Gambian women mentioned at the beginning of this chapter. Their positive inclination towards self-employment has a pragmatic quality: they have to earn money and they welcome almost any opportunity to do so. Income is the focus and not the activity or enterprise; this does not mean, that the positive-pragmatic woman is not interested in what she is doing. But she would prefer to have a safer source of income.

She generates this income for the family - or for herself if she lives alone - through self-employment or wage employment or a combination of both, because there is a need; her income constitutes an important, sometimes main part of the overall family income. One such example is Sadapili D. from Orissa, India:

> "Per month I earn 300 Rupees by selling liquor. Though my expenses for the house exceed this amount, I started saving five Rupees in the bank, with great difficulty. I have 190 Rupees in my name, now. This money will be my pillar of support in case of need, if someone asks, for my children's marriage. At such times, I need not borrow or worry. The habit of saving is a great improvement for our house and village."
>
> (Of the approximately two hundred enterprising women I have interviewed throughout the last years about half are either sole income earners or contribute the main or an equal share to the household income; the other half 'supplement' the income of the main earner(s). This 'supplement' is often used for school fees, or for clothing and school books for the children, or is saved for 'rainy days').
>
> Guchana P., another woman from Orissa, confirms the importance of saving: "I have acquired a new habit, that of saving. Out of the money I get from my daily work as a coolie I put a bit aside for rainy days. I already have 48 Rupees. These savings will enable me to stop borrowing from moneylenders... From now on, saving is part of my life."

The positive-pragmatic woman may have the opportunity to get occasional or seasonal wage-work, but it is inadequate to meet her real needs. She may never have worked before, especially if she is older, but is doing so now, because she has to: the husband left her or died or is very ill, the children still small or are not supportive.

For a Bangladeshi woman forty-five year old Nasma R. is quite old. Her husband is even older and is not able to work any longer, she said. They have three daughters all of whom they had married; but two came back because their husbands left them and now they sit at home without work and income. Nasma is worried, she cannot afford another two dowries. When I met her she worked in a road maintenance crew getting a minimum wage for a few hours work daily; some of that money was put on a bank account by the NGO that had organised this work for women like her. The road maintenance programme will be discontinued soon and the savings will be paid out to the women. And because there re no jobs, no employment opportunities, the NGO has encouraged the women to start a business. Most women want to buy chickens or a cow with this money but Nasma is planning to open a shop; she has never been 'in business' before but she hopes that her husband will help her somehow. "My family depends on me entirely", she said, looking very anxious, "keeping chickens alone would not help us". The other four women nodded; most of them are in similar conditions; two are widows, the two others have been abandoned by their husbands; Nasma is rather lucky to have a husband, even if is he not earning any income nowadays.

The income the positive-pragmatic woman earns comes from full-time self-employment, or from several part-time or micro activities and if need be she also takes up wage-work parallel to her enterprise activities.

Elisabeth S. is a German woman in her early thirties; her husband is a bus-driver and they have three children. Money is always short, but Elisabeth does not want her children to be left out of all the many school and after-school activities; she has always tried to earn some money in one way or another. Before her marriage, she had worked as a sales assistant in one of the large department stores in Frankfurt. When her youngest daughter started going to school, Elisabeth managed to get a part-time job in the same department store; she also caters for children's parties and is now thinking of starting a children's party service, which would also rent out games and toys, and organise magicians and other such entertainment.

This woman is not - cannot afford to be - too worried about what other people tell them a woman is allowed to do or not to do. She is usually involved in the kind of activities that women of her community do traditionally; she is also open to new ideas, but she does not have many ideas herself.

Isatou F. is a typical Gambian trader, selling beads and beauty products at Banjul main market. She is a trader, because that is what her people do. She went to school, but after some years her father said, it was time that she entered into business, because this is what their profession is, and not sitting in offices or such things.

"Being a business-person does not mean that you are bad or so", she said. "I don't feel people in general have a bad image of business people." But Isatou gave us this bit of information without being prompted; it must have been worrying her in some way.

Some of the product she sells she makes herself, like grinding some sort of turmeric powder; she also makes necklaces out of beads that she buys from other vendors.

Isatou would like to make more money but she does not know how. If we had any ideas, she would go into partnership with us, she suggested. But in general she believed that good business "is a matter of luck".

The positive-pragmatic woman needs the income, independent of whether other family members earn or do not earn. She has the support - moral and, if possible, financial - from her family who realises that her income is much needed, even if it is 'only' to save for her own marriage or that of her daughters.

If she has small children, she has managed to find income generating activities that can be done from home, because she has a specific skill. She has 'vernacular skills' or even 'non-traditional' skills that she uses for income generation. She is open to learning new skills, and she is good at improvising. Miriam M. from Colombia is one such woman:

Miriam M.'s husband Eustacio does not get drunk but he despairs so much more easily than Miriam. It may be that he married her because she is so strong; not only is she almost a head taller than he is and quite sturdy but she also has strong views of what is right and wrong, and if anything needs to be done she just does it while he keeps talking about it.

They met in 1966, when he was working as a gardener in one of the large cities of Colombia and she was a domestic helper in the same house. Already then she had clear ideas about her future, and so she asked her employer for a loan to buy a sewing machine. She wanted the machine "because one does not know what sort of husband one will get one day, and one must not rely on husbands anyhow. A sewing machine gives you economic independence". She got the loan, and bought the machine.

A year later she married Eustacio; soon after her employers left the country and she had to find other means of earning income. During the next eight years four children were born and Miriam earned most of the family income, by sewing for friends and neighbours. She started with mending clothes and doing alterations, eventually she taught herself how to make simple children's and women's clothes. When she had saved enough money to buy a refrigerator, she started a second 'business': selling cooled soft drinks and home-made ice-cream for people in the immediate neighbourhood. In this way, she earned about two thirds of the family income. The children grew up in a very small, three room house on the borderline between the city and one of the large slum areas, which the family bought with the help of a Government housing scheme.

All four of Miriam's children went to school and three have now gone on to college, studying computer science and foreign languages. Eustacio is still a gardener at the same place, with a tiny wage and with no hope of an old-age pension. Money has always been very tight, it showed when a year ago Miriam had to have an operation: there were no savings to speak of and as she could not earn for some time, they now do have severe financial problems. Miriam wishes she had a secure job!

The positive-pragmatic woman from a very poor background is likely to have work experience from early childhood on; poverty 'pushed' her into whatever she is doing and this is probably the same activity that she has done as a child, or that her mother or other family members have done before.

She has a strong social network of family and friends, and often she also belongs to a women's group or other 'development network'. If she is a member of a women's group enterprise, she is not the initiator of such groups; she belongs to such group or groups, because it is an alternative to employment.

Letwin M. from Zimbabwe is another typical positive-pragmatic woman. She is just thirty, has four children who are all still dependent; she lives in a village in Northern Zimbabwe. Her husband is an employee with a monthly income of around US$200. Letwin earn between US$100 and 150 monthly through various activities: she knits and sells sweaters; she makes and sells peanut butter; she has a small vegetable garden and sells some of its products and she is a member of a village women's co-operative. The women got together some years ago and decided to do something; someone had the idea of keeping bees as that does not require water and fertilisers and all those things that are scarce and difficult to get. They shared the work and began to earn a small income. But they feel that they still have lots of spare time and sit around too much, so they have now decided to get into oil-extraction and Letwin was sent to a training programme in food-processing, as none of the women has any knowledge in this field. They also hope that after the training programme they may be assisted to get a loan for their oil project.

I asked Letwin why she joined the co-operative. "One woman in the village had the idea", she said, "she is now the chairwoman; we others just went along; we need to earn money. Most women do that, they are forced to be self-employed because they need the money; their biggest problem are the unreliable husbands who often have several wives with families." "If you were offered a well paid job, would you give up your work in the co-operative?" I asked. "Yes, of course; but I would remain a member of the co-operative - you never know for how long you might be employed...".

Exposure to something new, to a new skill for example, or a new environment has increased the positive-pragmatic woman's perception of desirability or even of feasibility of enterprise. And so has financial support, if available. If such support is accessible to her, she will make use of it.

The positive-pragmatic woman is landless, and this has a major impact on her perception of desirability of enterprise, especially if she lives in a rural area: she would prefer to have her own land and earn a living from it.

Becoming empowered: The positive-ambitious woman

To be ambitious means to be strongly desirous *of* something or *to do* something. I use the word ambitious here in relation to the desire to be self-employed; it does not mean, that women of other types have no ambitions, but their ambitions are related to other things in life and not to enterprise. Among the women with a positive, ambitious inclination towards self-employment, some were not (yet) generating income from self-employment, but had a clear plan of action and were only constrained by lack of resources, usually capital. Compared with the uncertain women they did not say, for example, "if somebody would give the money" or "if somebody would tell me what to do" but they said "I can do it once I have got the money", and they were trying to convince friends to join them or a bank to give them a loan. Some of these women also joined women's savings groups the moment they were set up, because they saw the opportunity to get access to finance.

Other ambitious women I met *were* generating income - from very little to quite substantial sums - and wanted to invest all their efforts and resources in their activities; they wanted to see their businesses stabilise, grow or diversify.

"I would like to employ other women": The story of T.Manimala[11]

My father was a tailor throughout his life and stitched in his own house. From my early childhood I gave a helping hand to my father in his work. Earlier my father owned a machine. But towards the end of his life he was a poor man due to his extravagance and his alcoholic drinks. He died six years ago. We lived in a shabby little room paying monthly rent of thirty Rupees.

I am twenty three years old. I live with my mother and sister. For five years I stitched for "Praveen Tailors" who would bring the cut dresses to my house. He paid two Rupees fifty paise for one blouse. I watched keenly various designs and variety of methods of cutting the cloth at this shop. He gave me guidance willingly. To stitch certain garments like the long shirts worn by men lot of time and effort has to be put in and the amount paid is not proportionate. So from a year I have begun to take orders on my own.

I stitch very well. My speciality is ladies' and children's garments. I get lot of orders. During festivals I often stitch from five in the morning till eleven in the evening. On average I earn thirty to forty Rupees a day. However all money goes into daily expense. We buy the necessities according to the amount I earn each day. We may spend ten Rupees one day and twenty another day. I give all my income to my mother's hands. She buys the necessities for the house. We frequent the same shop for purchasing rice; so sometimes we buy on credit. When we get fifty or sixty Rupees at a time, we keep it aside for rent. We get our quota of kerosene from the ration shop. We use kerosene and coal for fuel. One tin of coal lasts for five days. Sometimes for the marriages and functions in our relatives' houses, we borrow money from others.

My mother is the only sister of six brothers. One brother had given her an old sewing machine during the division of the property. Three of her brothers are tailors here in Berhampur. Only one out of them is a little better off financially, as his daughter is helping him and his two sons are working in other shops.

After our father's death we stayed in our uncle's house for a year. He demanded two hundred Rupees a month as rent and a thousand Rupees as advance payment. So we shifted from there and lived in mother's cousin's place for four years, paying eighty Rupees a month.

My mother requested the wife of the owner of this house to give us some space. The lady took pity on her and said "You can come along with your daughters when we complete the construction of this house". So we came here a year ago. We pay two hundred and twenty a month as rent for the two little rooms, including water and electricity charges. We share the toilet with the owner's family.

My mother has very poor health. Always she suffers from blood pressure. Her eyes are also badly affected. Every now and then she has to consult the eye specialist at Giri Clinic, paying twenty or twenty five Rupees each time. She has to use eye drops every day. When we do not have money, the doctor does not force us to pay. When my sister or myself get sick, we go to Dr. Anand, who treated us from our childhood. We pay five Rupees for each visit. And he does not ask for more.

My sister is twenty years old. Her name is T.Manjula. She went to school up to class seven. Because of our poor economic condition and due to the belief, that girls should not go to school, my father stopped her education. She does all the household work, and she helps me whenever she finds time. But she does not have much interest in stitching.

I bought a tailoring machine on a bank loan from United Bank. We repay fifty Rupees each month. A year ago we bought a second-hand TV for 1,400 Rupees. For this we used the little savings we had in the savings account and took a loan of five hundred Rupees from United Bank on the guarantee of our savings account. We sold our old tailoring machine to the same person, to adjust the required amount. Last year we sold our old table fan and bought the ceiling fan. It cost us three hundred Rupees. For this reason we withdrew all the savings we had, one hundred fifty Rupees, from our savings account.

My mother is worried about getting both of us married. Dowry system is strict in our caste. Unless we possess some gold, other valuables and at least 10,000 Rupees no one will propose to marry. Staying in mother's house and working is not acceptable for a girl in our society. People think that a girl should get married, even though she may face hardships in her husband's house. If I marry, my mother and sister cannot carry on independently. And I cannot be certain, that my husband will look after them as well. So I wish that at least my sister should get married. However, I have no hopes to get her married, because of our poor economic condition.

*****

From my field research diary; my first visit to Manimala, after reading her story:

> "Many tailors I have seen are not very busy, have problems in getting orders. How is it that you have enough work?"
>
> "So many people know by now that I stitch very nicely; it spreads, there are many Gujaratis in this area, after my first Gujarati customer they seem to recommend me to others, although I do not belong to Gujarat; my father came from Andrah Pradesh."
>
> "How did you get your first customers?"
>
> "I started when I was 17 years old; first I worked for another tailor. Then I decided to work for myself after maybe four years. My first customer was a woman who knew me from my first job."
>
> "And why did you decide to work for yourself instead of being employed?"
>
> "Because then I had enough experience, I knew how to cut, how to stitch all kinds of things; I felt secure enough; also I thought I could earn more when working for myself."
>
> "How much do you charge for example for this blouse ?" (I pointed at the blouse she was stitching when we arrived).
>
> "For cutting and stitching a blouse I charge between seven and nine Rupees, it depends on the material; I also charge more if someone wants it done very quickly; and for very complicated designs I charge up to fifteen Rupees."
>
> "How many blouses can you do in one day?"
>
> "I could do seven blouses maximum in a day but most of the time I do four or five only. For a shalwar-kamiz [long shirt and trousers worn mostly by young women] I charge thirty Rupees; it takes about six hours to make."
>
> "What about plans for the future?"
>
> (the answer came very quickly) "I want a bigger tailor shop, I would like to have another machine or even more. I would also like to employ other women."
>
> "What hinders you from doing that?"
>
> "I would have to hire a larger room; one has to pay 10,000 Rupees advance payment these days, and then maybe five hundred monthly rent. I do not have that money yet."

Typical features of the positive-ambitious woman

It is not easy to find women like Manimala among women from poor a family background. There are, of course, poor women with an ambitious inclination towards self-employment, even among those who have never run an enterprise, but the ambition is very rarely achieved, because of all manner of constraints.

Malati S., from Orissa, is one such woman. She is a forty years old widow; her husband, to whom she was married as a child, died when she was still in her teens, leaving her without children. Malati has never been to school, but she is proud that she can write her name. She lives with her old and blind mother in her brother's house, sharing a room that is somehow an annex to the house and falling apart, the roof is leaking. Malati has just been cured from TB, is still very weak and can therefore not earn any money.

She had been 'good friends' with her brother, but the sister-in-law is bad, she said. The brother had become mean to her and her mother, and had more or less kicked them out of the house, saying that he could not feed them anymore. She and her mother had no other place to go to, so they were staying in that decaying annex. Her mother's monthly 'pension' of Rs 100 is their only income at the moment. If only she could earn some money, than she could give some to her brother and sister-in-law and they would not treat her so badly. Now she and her mother depended completely on their mercy. The brother has said several times: "Why are you eating our food?" Malati is desperate to get out of this situation.

Throughout the following discussion it became clear that she had a plan and had already collected some information about her 'project':

"What did you do before you got TB?"
"I was working as a coolie, a day-labourer."
"When you talked to Shanti the other day you said you want to start a vegetables business. Why that, why not something else?" [I mentioned the examples of what other women do or would like to do].
"When Shanti interviewed me and asked me what would I do to earn money, I could not think of anything else that day. It just came to my mind then. But I really would do anything, anything that is not too heavy physical work." Then she thought for a moment: "But papad making [which I had mentioned as one example] would not do, you cannot earn enough money to maintain yourself by making and selling papads", she said.
"How would your vegetable business be? Where would you sell?"

"I would sell in the house; I would also go to the weekly market on the cross-roads here."

"And where would you buy the vegetables, and who would go and buy them?"

"From the main, central market. I would go myself in the bus."

"There are surely a number of vegetable businesses here, a lot of women selling vegetables? Your will have to compete with them. Do you think you could earn enough money from that business to maintain yourself and your mother?"

"Yes, there are many women selling vegetables, but I can try." And then she got excited: What I would like to do most is start a peanut business. I know how to roast groundnuts. I have a friend who would like to go into partnership with me. There is some land in our village, it is no-man's land, we would like to grow nuts there. I can get the seed from my village. In my village they know all about it. Here it would be something new, you can't get roasted peanuts here, people would buy them. We have calculated that we need 2,000 Rupees to start that project."

"Why that amount?"

"To buy seed, to clean the land and pay somebody to take care, to guard the plants. Each of us would put in 1,000 Rupees. But we don't know how to get money; I do not have that money. I had some savings from when I used to do day-labour but I have given all to my brother. Now he is treating me like that. I don't even have a house of my own."

"And what about the vegetable business? Would you want to do that in addition to the peanut business?"

"That I would only start if I cannot get the money for the peanut business."

Two months later Malati had helped to start the first women's savings group in her community and had been selected as the group's secretary.

The ambitious woman invests great effort into starting a very specific, self-employed activity or into expanding or diversifying her existing enterprise.

The woman with an ambitious inclination can be of any age, but if she has succeeded, she is likely to be middle-aged. Her family is not against her enterprise activities; a husband, if he is around at all, does either not interfere, or has joined in the business after some time, mostly after it has become more successful. Often enhough, he is using the businesses' cash box to pay for his personal expenses, in other words, is being a nuisance.

Bintou C. runs a food-stall in Brikama, on the road to The Gambia's main airport. She makes sandwiches filled with meat-stew, fish-balls or beans; these three 'sauces' are prepared by herself. The stall is on one of the main roads and during the one hour or so we spent with her around lunch time, the business was extremely good.

She sells a whole baguette for twelve Dalassis, a quarter for three and an eighth for one fifty. She works very fast, cutting the bread and filling it, wrapping it in bits of paper. The paper usually some old newspaper or old brown packing paper. Her stall has a roof and her basins with food are covered with plates all the time to keep the flies out. People know what they can buy from her, she does not have to show it.

Her business runs all the year round, from morning until she has sold whatever she had prepared. She could sell more but it would be too strenuous. She does it to keep her family, that is herself and her two children, going; her first husband died, his brother married her but is not living with her. He contributes only a little bit towards the household expenses.

Previously she used to roast peanuts and sell them to school children but when schools are closed there is no business, so she changed to this business.

Two of her sisters are selling at the same stall, but each works independently; it would be too difficult to do it jointly; it depends on the size of the family how much each woman can contribute; it is also a question of mentality, she said.

She is illiterate but would like to learn to read and write; she wants her business to develop, she thinks there is growth potential for her business but she has no idea how to make better sales apart from investing more time which she cannot do. The family demands are high, she cannot re-invest money in the business but needs whatever she makes to keep the family.

Her younger sister sometimes helps, and so do other family members. But her husband only asks her for money from the business without ever repaying; "this problem is rampant" she said, and her sister, working next to her, agreed vehemently.

In rural areas, the ambitious woman will not easily give up her agricultural activities for the sake of her enterprise, even though she wants this enterprise to prosper. More than an urban woman, she depends on other income and resources, because the market for the kind of products or services she can offer, is local and small.

Naranga P., a landless tribal woman from Orissa, has worked as a coolie or agricultural labourer for most of her life, and most of her cash income even now comes from this type of work. But she is also involved in many things in her village. Together with four other women she is running a small 'shop'. Their monthly earnings after costs are about 150 Rupees from selling rice and 100 Rupees from other items. So far they have reinvested every rupee to buy new items and expand their range of products. Customers also come from other villages; there are very few shops in this area.

The women also make candles and extract honey, both for home-consumption. "How is it", I asked her, "that you are involved in so many things, how can you find time for all this?" "I want to help more women here, now that I know how to talk and how to lead a group". "And what is your dream for yourself?" "I would like the shop to grow, working together with the other women"; but then, after a while she said: "What I really want is my own shop!"

The woman who has succeeded, comes from communities where livelihood activities and enterprise are part of life, either because of poverty or because of tradition; this has influenced her positive perception of enterprise.

She may have a few years of formal education, but this is not central to her inclination or actual activity. Her enterprise is based on her 'domestic' or 'vernacular' skills, often acquired in previous employment or wage work.

Poonaman C. has a well-established ready-made garments business. She started this business about twenty years ago and has always only made shirts and blouses of various styles, and of average quality of material but very good finish. She employs about twenty piece-rate workers, all women. A skilled out-worker can make up to three shirts per day. She has trained many of these women herself.

Twenty years ago she was a piece-rate worker herself, working in a garment factory; but the earnings were not enough. So one day she decided to go into business. From her savings she paid the first instalment for a sewing machine. She started making a few shirts which she took to retailers to sell them; at the beginning she was able to sell only small quantities. Now she sells between 50 to 200 shirts a day, depending on the season; her customers are middlemen and retailers in Chiangmai; she has more than ten regular customers nowadays.

Poonaman C. has become a real business woman; her suppliers of raw materials give her thirty to forty-five days credit. She does a proper costing of the finished products and adds between five and ten Bhat per shirt as her profit margin. What about competition? "Oh, yes, competitions is there and it is quite fierce; but I have established good relationship with my customers and they know they can rely on me, on the quality of my shirts and the timeliness of our deliveries".

Her husband used to work as a driver. When she started the business he was against it. "I did not pay any attention ... and I won", she says and smiles. He lost his job because the company closed down and she taught him how to cut material. When he got bored with cutting he started searching for outside employment. "I told him he can't do that", she remembers, "we had too many orders." Now he drives the goods: orders and materials to the out-workers, finished goods to the customers.

They are doing well; they own a house, with solid furniture and all sorts of appliances and facilities; they own a car; and their two children are going to university. Poonaman and her husband went only to primary school, for a few years. Compared to most of their neighbours they are indeed well-off. And plans for the future? "Well", she says, "I would like this business to grow but we are happy that we are doing relatively well, compared to so many others. My sister-in-law has a similar business but she is struggling because she does not have a clear business line; she is making too many different products; that does not work."

The full-time enterprise of the ambitious woman is related to a traditional female occupation (for example tailoring or food processing); this is an area where she feels confident.

Lucy G. started her fruit business in November 1993. She had had a job as a receptionist in an office in Nairobi but it was "not a proper job" and she had too many problems, too much frustration in combining it with her duties as a mother of three. So she decided to start something of her own.

She had used her own savings to start dealing in old clothes but there was too much competition. Never-the-less, she managed again to save some money and decided to try something different: selling fruits. She rented the small, simple stall, located in an open market next to the General Hospital. When she realised that everybody here was doing the same she tried selling fresh passion fruit juice. First is did not go well, some people had never tried such juice. She convinced customers not to buy soda water or soft drinks but a fresh juice instead because it is healthier. Now she also sells orange juice during the orange season. She makes the juices at home but she does not have a blender and the making of passion fruit juice is therefore a lengthy process. Her dream is to have a blender; but the cheapest costs about 5,500 Kenyan Shillings, and she does not have that money.

After the juices she introduced fruit salad. She prepares it in her stall every day. The salad consists of papaya, passion fruit and pineapple and she sells a bowl (two large serving spoons) for twenty Shillings. She also adds banana slices and/or avocado slices to the salad if people ask for it but then she charges two Shillings more. On cold days she may sell only ten such bowls, in summer more. She also sells half a bowl (she does not have the money to buy small cups) for ten Shillings and she keeps some recycled plastic containers with lids (e.g. large margarine pots) for people who want to take the salads into the hospital. Usually people come and eat their salad in her little stall. Behind the counter she has two small benches along the walls that can sit up to four people.

To attract customers she had first charged fifteen Shillings per bowl of salad; but then people told her that it is so good and that she should charge more. A woman who was eating a salad while we were sitting inside Lucy's stall told us that downtown one would have to pay thirty Shillings for a bowl of fruit salad. The reason for her price being still low is that a packet of crisps costs twenty Shillings and Lucy realised that the man selling crisps is her greatest competitor.

Her sister-in-law helps her to run the business; she pays her a salary. But she does not pay herself a salary because so far she cannot afford it. The rent of the stall is high: 1,200 Shillings; but the owner gives her credit. She also buys some of the fruits on credit. The bananas, for example, she buys from a nice woman who used to have a stall like hers and whose business has grown into a retail business. The woman trusts her and even supplies the bananas. In return, if the business is going well Lucy sometimes pays the woman in advance. Papayas she gets from somebody who brings them from outside Nairobi. In this way she only pays 700 instead of 1,200 Shillings per crate from a retailer; but this supplier does not come regularly and so sometimes she has to buy papayas even from neighbouring stalls in order to keep her fruit salad customers happy.

Lucy's main problem is transport. She has to take public transport and that is often a problem because some fruits are delicate. She has to hire a carrier who will charge some sixty Shillings to carry a big sack of oranges from the market to the bus. Sometimes she hires a car, especially if she has to buy papayas at the market.

Another problem is water. There are water pipes but her stall does not have a tap and there is no tap nearby so she has to hire small boys to bring fresh water to wash cups, bowls and spoons. The water is kept in a bucket underneath her sales counter (and fruit display) and she keeps two or three washing up bowls there, too.

Her dream is to have a proper shop where she can sell a variety of fruits and juices. Even to have a better market stall would be great; but the rent for a stall in the larger, covered markets is about 1,800 or 2,000 Shillings which she can not yet afford.

If an ambitious woman has a single, full-time enterprise, she spends most of her time in her business in order to make a living; in this case she is not actively involved in women's or community groups' activities. But those women, whose enterprises occupy only part of their time, are very likely to be involved in women's groups activities, because these group activities are important for their enterprising as well as their personal and social ambitions; the ambitious woman is likely to be the leader or one of the leaders of such a group.

> Like Bharati A. from Orissa: She is a young mother of about thirty years of age. Her husband, three children, mother- and sister-in-law live in a small, two room house in a slum resettlement area. With a monthly income of around 1,200 Rupees they are among the 'lucky', better off people of this settlement; but this 'luck' may be temporary: Her husband is a 'temporary peon' in a school. At the moment her husband is, thus, the main income earner. Bharati works in a tailoring training centre for three hours every day, training other young women. She was once a trainee there herself and had then managed, with the help of the Centre, to get part-time employment in a small tailoring shop. The shop had closed down after six months but she had been lucky enough to get this other part-time job. Her husband's earnings alone would not be sufficient to feed a family of seven, although she earns a few Rupees extra every month by sewing blouses for women of the neighbourhood whenever she can get hold of one of the sewing machines of the training centre.
> When I first met Bharati she talked about her ambition to have her own tailoring business; but she did not have a sewing machine or the means to buy one. If only her husband could keep his job as a peon, she might be able to save. Then, a few months later, the idea of setting up a women's saving and credit group was created and Bharati, being one of the founding members, was elected chairwoman. Apart from hoping to get access to money for a sewing machine this way, she also thought it a very good idea: "Women in this community do not earn income because they don't have the means to earn and, what is more, they lack proper guidance", she said.

Although employment for women is scarce, the ambitious woman is among those, who would be able to get employment - in fact she has been employed in one way or the other; but she prefers to be independent and be her own boss.

References and Notes

[1] "In times of need women get busy ... and men get drunk" was a forceful sentiment expressed by a Zambian business woman

[2] ILO = International Labour Organisation

[3] UNIFEM = United Nations Development Fund for Women

[4] Berger, 1989, p.1

[5] see for example Menefee Sing and Kelles-Viitanen, 1987

[6] see Jhabvala and Tate, 1996

[7] see for example Jumani, 1991

[8] see Dignard and Havet, 1995

[9] ibid, p.9

[10] When my husband's daughter saw the title (Getting down to business) of a training manual for women entrepreneurs that we had produced, she burst out in laughter. We, in our naiveté, had not been aware of the double meaning of our title. Yet for thousands of women all over the world this specific 'getting down' is indeed - sad as it may be - a very pragmatic means of feeding their children or whole families.

[11] The custom of putting the initial of the 'family' name before the name is used in Southern Orissa and Andrah Pradesh.

4 Changing perceptions of enterprise

Two sets of learning

I have often thought about going into business myself, because I feel it would increase my credibility for the subject that I teach and write about most. I am now self-employed, because it gives me the flexibility that I need to run a fairly busy household and to pursue other interests. I can afford not to have a regular, monthly income - I have a husband who does. But I do not consider myself as being a 'business woman' or an 'entrepreneuse' and I do not seem to have enough courage, and probably no real need, to make the step from being a self-employed, professional woman to running a business.

If a woman is poor one could assume, that because she needs money, she has no choice but to pluck up the courage that I am lacking and to get involved in enterprising activities. One could also assume, that if a job offers nothing but very low payment and bad treatment, a woman would try her very best to find a better way of earning money, even if it is not very much more money. Yet we have seen in the previous chapters, that many women do not try. So, what is it that makes some 'get down to business', even become successful and others not? What else is necessary apart from the intrinsic personal characteristics which are, as I have said in the introduction, outside my domain.

When I looked more closely at all the cases I had collected within each of the five types of women and compared them, I found that change of some sort was happening or had happened in the attitude of some women of each type, either during the time of my field research or in the women's past. It had not happened to all women: many of the uncertain women, for example, seemed to 'dream' forever about self-employment, but never got down to doing it. Yet there were a number of positive cases where women had moved on, from being despondent to being more confident, and were considering the possibility to doing something new, which could be employment or self-employment. Or they had moved on, from being uncertain to becoming 'positive-pragmatic', or even 'ambitious' women. And while some women had moved on on their own account, changes of other women's situations had been initiated by outsiders.

The ambiguous title of this chapter refers to two sets of learning: that a woman's perception of enterprise as being something that *she* can do (or she *can* do) changes, when certain conditions around her have changed, and that this change can, to a certain degree, be initiated by outside intervention. These points as such are obvious. What is not quite so obvious is: what actually has to happen for women to move on? From the women I learned, that to change their perceptions (and for us 'development interventionists' to be able to change women's perceptions), more than mere economic opportunities (such as the opportunity to get a loan, or to have a product which can be sold) have to come to pass.

I would like to add of word on methodology here. The differences and changes that I found among the women of the five types are, of course, not only based on written life stories and other written materials that I collected throughout many field visits and working assignments. They are also based on the very personal impression that each woman made and that is stored somewhere in the labyrinth of my brain, mingling there with memories of sounds, smells, laughter, desperation, a sudden smile, a brief sparkle in the eyes of an otherwise sombre-looking face, and with memories of earlier experiences, and of other women and men. Any judgement about the women's personalities comes not from psychological tests, but from these my personal impressions. I trusted my age and experience to filter out what was essential and was, therefore, to go into the 'lessons learned' messages that I have included in this chapter.

In the following five sections I analyse, what has happened to the women of the five types who have - or have not - moved on. All the women mentioned here - unless stated otherwise - have been introduced in the two previous chapters but the "List of Women" at the end of this book (pages 128-130) may help you to remember some details about these women.

Each section also contains a few 'lessons for development intervention' that I learned from the women, from analysing and comparing their cases. None of these lessons are particularly original or new, but most of them may need to be communicated to a wider public as well as the development community, in order that they may be discussed, and that they get a greater chance of being implemented. It is not my intention to give recipes, but to stimulate awareness of poor women's needs regarding their capabilities and opportunities for income generation. The diagrams on the following five pages summarise the main characteristics of the five types of women presented in the previous two chapters, and the issues that will be discussed in this chapter.

Typical features:

- does not find self-employment desirable or feasible
- belongs to the poorest of the poor
- has small children
- has plenty of time to spare due to poverty
- is isolated within her community

Type:

> **NEGATIVE-DESPONDENT WOMAN**
> (see pages 28-35)

Primary needs:

- 'charity' to get out of destitution
- the support of a women's group

Change:

Moving out of Despondency
(see pages 88-92)

| Negative-Pragmatic | Positive-Uncertain | Positive Pragmatic |

Typical features:

- finds self-employment desirable but not feasible
- someone in the family is earning but it is not sufficient
- has small children
- lacks confidence in own abilities
- does not have marketable skills

|

Type:

**POSITIVE-UNCERTAIN
WOMAN**
(see pages 36-44)

|

Primary needs:

- to realise the strength of being a woman
- access to child-care facilities
- marketable skills

|

Change:

Becoming certain
(see pages 93-102)

| |

Positive-   Positive-
Pragmatic   Ambitious

Typical features:

- finds self-employment undesirable
- has found fairly regular but badly paid wage-work
- family depends on her income
- does not have time to spare due to double burden of work and household

Type:

**NEGATIVE-PRAGMATIC
WOMAN**
(see pages 50-58)

Primary needs:

- to belong to a 'trade union'

Change:

Gaining security
(see pages 103-105)

Typical features:

- finds self-employment to be a feasible way of earning money
- would prefer to be employed or have her own land
- is involved in various activities to make ends meet
- is involved in women's groups or other 'networks'
- does not (yet) have access to financial services

Type:

POSITIVE-PRAGMATIC WOMAN (see pages 59-68)

Primary needs:

- to have access to loans
- a plot of land
- to have access to employment

Change:

Becoming ambitious
(see pages 106-112)

Positive-Ambitious

Typical features:

- is self-employed or has very concrete business idea
- has marketable skills
- family is supportive
- is better off than other poor women
- has work experience

|
∇

Type:

```
┌─────────────────────────────────┐
│      POSITIVE-AMBITIOUS          │
│            WOMAN                 │
│        (see pages 69-79)         │
└─────────────────────────────────┘
```

|

Primary needs:

- experience and exposure

|
∇

Change:

From ambition to success
(see pages 113-118)

Moving out of despondency

In chapter two I presented the short cases of three 'negative-despondent' women from India: Moti, Preeti and Prabha. Their stories show, that poverty is not only about the inability to attain a minimal standard of living. While all are very poor, Prabha is certainly the poorest of them; Preeti's and Moti's families do have the means for one meal or more a day, and they do have a roof over their heads, which many people, especially in the large cities of India and Bangladesh, do not have. But poverty is not only about the physical consequences of not having the economic means to buy food, decent shelter and all that. It is also, as I have discussed in chapter two, about powerlessness, isolation, about the inability to cope, and to pull oneself out of the situation. Moti, Preeti and Prabha seem to be caught in the "deprivation trap".

For a woman the "deprivation trap" can be intensified by the mere fact of her gender, more so in societies where the status of women is very low. This seems to work on two levels: a social and economic level, with isolation, powerlessness and all the other factors that make the "deprivation trap"; and a psychological level with the woman's own assumption of being a lesser being, through which the actual powerlessness and isolation are reinforced and internalised. Preeti is a good example for this; while her brother-in-law (who is poor but better off than many other people in India, and on whom Preeti is dependent) can go out and work in his miserable 'workshop', Preeti herself is caught in the trap: all the categories of deprivation apply to her to a much greater degree than to her brother-in-law.

Nothing is feasible in the perception of a woman in this condition. Yet under certain circumstances her perception of life, her 'grip on life' can change, can become more positive. In respect to enterprise, she is then likely to become one of the many positive-pragmatic women, who run micro-enterprises in every corner of the world, because the employment, or the plot of agricultural land she may prefer as a source of income, is not accessible for her.

At the end of my field research, Preeti seemed to have started to move out of despondency. In her life-story she had said things like "I do not know how to carry on living" and "...in my situation I am unable to make any personal plans". But once she had told this story, and Girija, a young, active woman in her community to whom she told it, had talked to her several times, her perception seemed to be changing. She had dared to join a group of young women in her neighbourhood who had started (without the intervention of an outside organisation) to get together to talk and to do things together. Preeti was now mentioning the possibility of working in the 'chocolate factory' (a small home enterprise producing sweets and employing several young women as wage workers) in her neighbourhood.

Another example is Sadapili D., who had moved out of despondency and had become a positive-pragmatic woman. When she first told me her story, her despondency came out clearly through statements like "I am fed up with life and I do not have any more mental or physical strength, to do coolie work or shifting cultivation. You help me! How can I bring up my children?" But then the women's group in her village started a silk-worm project with the help of a local voluntary organisation, and she got involved, although she would still prefer to have a secure job as a peon.

What had changed these two women's negative perception of self and life in general, was a group of women of their own community and background, who had shown them a way out of despondency. Among a group of women Preeti and Sadapili had started to moved out of isolation and powerlessness. What is important, though, is that compared to Prabha both women had already secured their very basic needs (regular food, a roof over their head).

Why has Prabha not moved out? Because she has small children and she has no means to feed her children and herself, except through fairly regular, humiliating begging; when she goes out begging, she can take her children, even involve them in begging. Prabha is despised by most of her neighbours and is isolated within her community. And Moti? She, too, has small children and she is fairly isolated within her village; she does not belong to any women's group, because her family does not like it and maybe because other women in the existing group think she is lazy. She depends completely on her husband's irregular and insufficient contributions to the household, for food, for repairing the roof, for everything, and she worries about it. It is as if this worry paralyses her whole life.

I have learned two main lessons from these women:

- that there must be room for charity, and
- that despondent women need the support of a women's group.

These two lessons are discussed below.

Lesson 1:   There must be room for charity

Before a despondent woman changes her negative perception of self and life in general, she needs a roof and some regular food for her children and herself. A famous Chinese proverb (transferred to a woman) says "If you give a woman a fish she will eat it and be hungry again tomorrow; if you teach a woman how to fish she will be able to maintain herself and her family". It is wise, but needs to be looked at from a gender perspective. Before the woman can hold a fishing rod or net, she needs the physical strength to do so, she needs, to use a technical language, a certain minimum intake of calories of food. The woman is also likely to have small children; the poorer the woman, the more likely this is. With two or more little hungry children around her, it is difficult for her to hold the fishing rod and sit by the river, patiently waiting for the fish that will feed her and these children. This woman may need charity of a specific kind while she is being taught to fish.

Charity derives from the Greek word kharis meaning favour or grace; according to the *Concise Oxford Dictionary* charity can mean "giving voluntarily to those in need"; "kindness, benevolence"; "tolerance in judging others" or "love of one's fellow men". Nowadays it is sadly associated with handouts, dependence, helplessness, even getting an 'easy ride'. Charity is, thus, a difficult concept loaded with all sorts of images and expectations, and there is an increasing call for taking a 'business approach' to charitable acts: "Let them pay for it"; "Give loans, not gifts".

I believe, that charity is about giving someone the opportunity to get out of a serious difficulty. I remember how important "CARE Pakete", that is parcels sent by the charity CARE from the United States, containing food and clothing, were for us German children immediately after the second world war. Without charity, many Jewish people and other "unwanted subjects" - as socialists, gays, gypsies and other minorities were called in Nazi Germany - who managed to escape the Nazi regime, would not have been able to survive and begin a new life. Without charity, in this case cash given regularly by a group of people, the fifty girls of a small boarding school in India would have to be sent back to a future of prostitution and leprosy. We all know of examples of such meaningful charitable acts.

Neither Preeti nor Prabha need charity money handed out to them, but an income generating activity (such as a fish pond for which they would require training) on the other hand, set up in their community by a charitable organisation, would not be of help to them either. Prabha would not know where to leave her children, and Preeti would not be allowed to join in. Nor would joining a savings and credit scheme enable Prabha to get money quickly to repair the damages to her roof.

What both women need are "charitable" services, free of charge and given voluntarily and with kindness and especially with "tolerance in judging others". A sheltered home for beaten and abandoned women like Prabha, or roofing materials and a helping hand for her to repair her leaking roof and make her hut inhabitable; free but reliable child-care for her three small children, so that she can set her mind and time to find a job or join an enterprising group; food for the time of training for the job or activity; free and empathetic family counselling services, provided by *professional* counsellors, preferable of her own community, for her and for Preeti (and her brother-in-law) on various aspects of day-to-day and future life. Many so-called developing countries, especially in South-Asia, have a large number of such charitable services, and India especially has thousands of wonderful people, who are willing to 'give a helping hand' to people in distress. Very poor people, though, especially women, often do not know about these services or believe they are not entitled to get them.

Charity is, thus, ideally about helping someone out of a serious difficulty; charity for destitute, 'ultra-poor' women is about helping them over the first, most difficult hurdle onto a path that leads out of despondency and into self-reliance.

Lesson 2: Despondent women need the support of a women's group

Belonging to a group of women from a similar background gives a woman more confidence to break the "deprivation gap". To take the Chinese saying of the fish and the fishing again: The woman also needs to see - to become aware - that it is only custom, but not moral or other law, that restrains a woman from taking up a traditionally male occupation like fishing. Once she has gained this awareness, she needs the psychological strength to convince her traditional community, her family and peers of the same, because otherwise the family or community will exert its control function and make sure, that she moves within the prescribed boundaries of her gender and class or caste. This may mean, that although she herself has realised, that she can take up fishing, her community will prevent her from doing it by punishing her. The punishment can take many forms, it can be slow and covert, but it will either bring the woman back into 'line' or force her to leave, which will be almost impossible for her, if she has small children.

If the woman belongs to a group of women, the process of becoming aware is easier; not that the group can do the mental work for the woman, but the individual women whose 'eyes are opening' encourage and reinforce each others' process of learning.

I have experienced this process within my own self. For some thirty years of my life I lived the life of an individualist; I felt that I was an 'emancipated woman' and that my struggles with men and with work primarily had to do with myself, my own incompetence. I blamed myself for failing in many things, privately and in my work. Then, by chance, I began working with women, began reading about women, talking to women, became a member of two women's groups. Slowly, I became aware, that many of my 'problems' had to do with the way I had been brought up, with being a woman. I am not now blaming my parents or men in general for it, but I have realised, that my failures have had to do with half-hearted ways of approaching things ("*I* cannot really do this, can I?" and "If I do this, I will not have enough time for 'him', the family, the household"); or not setting priorities and always feeling that social matters, that other human beings come first ("Of course you can leave your children here, I'm around anyhow"; "No, no, don't take a taxi, I can take you to that meeting, I have nothing important going on tomorrow"). Knowing that other women, all over the world, face similar problems, has helped me to gain strength, has empowered me to say 'no' at least sometimes. It has also helped me to feel easy about certain 'failures', because I realised, that they are only failures in a male world of competition.

What has happened to me, I have seen happening to many women. And it can happen - must happen - to Preeti and Prabha and other despondent and uncertain women. Imagine Preeti and her sister saying "no" to her brother-in-law. What would he do, what could he do? Nothing much; one man can only beat one woman, not two. And much less three or four Belonging to a group increases women's confidence and their potential for action.

In modern language, the informal group of family, friends, peers is the 'social network'. A group of people of one's own profession, or of relevance to one's work, is the 'professional network'. These days we do not visit people for a chat or an exchange of experiences, we do it for 'networking' and those who do not network, lose out on opportunities; this is certainly true for people's choices of work, of a 'career', and of the development of that career.

Social networks play an important role in our career choices and developments because they provide[1]
- information (such as about schools, training programmes, how to get admitted somewhere; about potential job and business opportunities),
- sponsorship and support (such as informal loans to learn a skill; informal capital to start or expand a business),
- credibility (for example introduction to an employer or a bank manager by a friend, but also
- control (that is standards of behaviour acceptable to the community).

Preeti, Prabha or Moti do not have the benefits of a group or network and this may be partly because of their communities' 'standards of behaviour'. Preeti, for example had allegedly been seen going off with men, prostitution was not mentioned but implied ("she's a bad woman"); that she may have done it because she needed food for her children and herself, did not make her into a less bad woman in the eyes of others. Moti is considered to be lazy by some people; it may be that she is, but the story she told me sounded as though her 'laziness' had to do with being paralysed by the circumstances of her life.

Preeti, Prabha and Moti belong to those women, who would need group support most. Yet they did not even have the support of what could be call an "artificial network",[2] a set-up of people and organisations to support them. Voluntary and other development organisations would be part of such an artificial network; voluntary organisation are increasingly involved in setting up or using existing women's groups for all kind of purposes. People working in such organisations have to be able to uncover latent social problems (for example to uncover why certain women are excluded from group activities and even from social networks), to make them into obvious ones (for example present the problem to the other women in those groups) and if necessary to assist in finding solutions.

Becoming certain

How does a woman with a positive, but uncertain inclination towards enterprise become certain that she wants to, or is able to start her enterprise? In Chapter Two I presented Santilata, Yanjuke, Urmila and Helen as examples of typical positive-uncertain women.

Santilata has three children, one of them is an infant. Her husband's income is very low and that is the main reason why Santilata needs to (and sometimes used to) earn money. Now she has a baby which she cannot leave anywhere, so self-employment seems to her to be a good solution. But she does not have any skills with which she could produce something from home.

Yanjuke does not have children, but like Santilata she, too, does not have any skills that she could use to produce anything during the tourist off-seasons. And Helen? She does not seem to have any particular skills and ten years or more ago she was stranded, because she did have a small child in a fairly remote village; she is still 'stuck' because she is caught in a typical gender trap: because she looked after her child and found cleaning jobs near her home, for many years she did not venture out to find anything better. Now she is 'out', she has no experience in doing anything else. Urmila does have a skill, but she is, like Helen, stuck in the house of her brothers. She does not really dare to set off on her own, does not believe she can do it on her own.

How do these uncertain women compare with positive-pragmatic ones like, for example, Miriam and Letwin?

Miriam, too, had small children when she first started earning an income; but she had a skill - which she had taught herself - *and* a tool (a sewing machine) to turn this skill into cash income - at home; she had been able to buy the machine with an interest free loan, which she got from her employer. In development slang this means: she had access to resources. And there is, no doubt, something in Miriam's personality, that has helped her to earn money: she is a confident and outgoing woman who knows many people in her neighbourhood.

Letwin is another similar example: she has four dependent children, but she knew how to knit and how to make peanut butter; she also has the support of a women's cooperative, through which she can market some of her home-made products, and she, like Miriam, appeared to me and others as a woman who is confident and knows her own worth.

The comparison of these and other women taught me, that if we want to encourage and assist "uncertain" women to become self-employed, we need to consider the following:

- to make women aware of the strength of their gender;
- to provide child-care facilities, and
- to teach women marketable skills.

Lesson 3: *Show women the strength of their gender*

It was Miriam, thirty years ago, who gave me my first lesson in "gender awareness". We were talking about children and birth control, Pope Paul VI had just announced his encyclica Humanae Vitae. Miriam was angry; she came from a community of poor families with many children; poverty was preventing many of these children from having any real chance of a life in decency, to have a life beyond infancy or early childhood at all. "The pope is committing a large sin" she, a true Catholic woman, said. "He has no right to impose child birth on women, he is a man, he does not know what it means to have one child after the other ... fathered by drunken men ". And it was Miriam who later bought herself a sewing machine, because although she wanted to get married, she thought it would not be wise to rely on a husband. Miriam has succeeded, she has brought up four children to a level never achieved before neither in her family nor among other people of her village.

From early childhood Miriam had been forced to earn an income; as a young girl she came to work for a liberal family. She learned, that she was a human being of equal worth with others around her, with wealthier people, foreigners, with men, because she was given the same respect. So together with economic independence she developed an independent spirit, pride in being a woman and confidence in her own abilities.

Neither Yanjuke nor Helen are confident in their own abilities. Like Preeti and Moti they seem to be waiting for 'somebody' or something to take charge and show them the way. They confirm what Colette Dowling[3] wrote many years ago:

> "Fear, irrational and capricious - fear that has no relation to capabilities or even to reality - is epidemic among women today. ... Phobia has so thoroughly infiltrated the feminine experience, it is like a secret plague. ... and is all the more insidious for being so thoroughly acculturated we do not even recognise what has happened to us. ... Women will not become free until they stop being afraid."

This 'phobia' may be an explanation for the often negative feedback that I have received from colleagues running gender training programmes. Gender training has been included in many development programmes as a strategy to create awareness among development policy makers and development workers; I have conducted such programmes myself. Most of these programmes seemed to use similar concepts, contents and methodologies. One of my Indian colleagues, for example, conducted some thirty gender training programmes for staff of local, small voluntary organisations during the last two years. She reported, that men were, on the whole, more open to the issues discussed during these workshops, and that she had to deal with a lot of resistance, even hostility from many of the women. Her assessment of this situation was, that the women were afraid of change, partly because they knew that once they were back in their villages, introducing anything new would be difficult and would encounter a lot of resistance from men and from women.[4]

Gender analysis, about which one typically learns in a gender training programme, has threatening aspects for men *and* for women. Women know, that they work more hours than men; they know, that they may have the use of, but not the power over their husbands' resources (a house, land, tools, equipment) and that they own much less than their husbands, to the degree of being completely dependent; they know, that they may be the ones who clean the church and organise the church fete, but that that only brings recognition to the usually male priest and other usually male leaders. Women, poor and rich, often complain about these issues. What they may not know or rather, may not want to know, is that this situation can be changed and that they themselves are the only ones, who can bring about this change.

Gender training, at least of the kind that is known to me, may be useful to create a certain amount of awareness among development planners and workers. But it needs more than a training programme, to strengthen women's awareness of their own abilities and opportunities, and to encourage women to become their own persons, to take responsibility for their own lives. It needs exposure to possibilities, positive experiences, positive feedback. It may need a 'critical event' to set something in motion within the woman; or a 'push' from someone who has the confidence of the woman. Like Naranga P., who ten years ago was a very poor, landless coolie and is now a member of the local village council. Sasi Prabha, the woman who has 'pushed' Naranga, told me how it all developed:

> "First we went to the villages to discuss liquor problems: making people aware that they should spend money for food and not for liquor; after that, we started with community awareness programmes in many villages, leadership training; then the problems of landless people, we managed to convince the local government to give land to landless people; then came the housing programme, to build new houses in the villages or improve the existing ones by putting better roofs and such things; some villages also got

gobar-gas. After that, I started a sort of women's awareness programme, going around the villages, sitting somewhere where people would gather and inviting them to discuss with me; then we took up women's health education and nutrition. We also encouraged the women to ask for higher wages, equal wages with the men. After all that we went round asking the women: do you want to earn additional income? Then we offered skills training; each village was asked to select women for the training..." "Was it difficult to convince people, especially men, to let the women go ahead?" "We did have to do a bit of 'brainwashing'", she says laughing, "you know, pushing for decisions, talking, convincing. Then women began to realise that it works, that they can set something in motion...".

Lesson 4: *Women need child-care services*

Bringing up children is one of the most, if not the most important aspect of any society and is central to the individuals involved in it: the children, the parents, the extended family, but essentially the woman: the mother. In all societies child-care is seen as a mother's duty and even in the most 'advanced' societies there is at least a feeling of guilt, when a mother leaves her young child in a crèche or kindergarten to go for work or just to have a few hours to herself, often spent on other 'reproductive' duties. Providing adequate child-care facilities is rarely given the priority it deserves.

I cannot imagine anyone needing child-care facilities more than Prabha or, at least at times, Santilata, yet they are the ones who have the least access to it, and if it is available, it is mostly of low quality. And more than that: neither the society they live in, nor their immediate communities encourage such facilities; there is a stigma attached to any woman who does not look 'properly' after her own children.

The view that a mother is the best person for a small child to be with may be right, but does not reflect the social reality of most women nowadays. In a few traditional societies men and women still have their specific tasks, women are actively involved in subsistence activities such as working the land, processing food for home consumption, tending animals, and these subsistence activities are recognised and valued for what they are: indispensable work; hard but satisfying and even dignifying work. Children can be around, can be kept close, and are often required to contribute their important share to the livelihood of the family.

For most women, for millions of women around the world, life is not so 'idyllic': they are landless, they live in tiny huts or rooms in impoverished villages or city slums, often without an extended family network. Money is needed for survival, and this money can only be earned by working for an employer or being self-employed. If a woman has infants, her hands are tied and she depends on the small, seasonal or irregular income of her husband, if he lets his family have a fair share of it. She may be able to set up some small business activity from home or near to home, or to get some irregular work, where she can carry her baby on her back with her. Or she may have a daughter, who is old enough to look after the infant/s; this daughter will not go to school, and will soon grow up into a life like that of her mother. If the woman does not have any idea or skill or the money needed to start a home-based business, she might be able to get at least some casual labour to earn the cash that would make the little difference to her and her children's life - *if* she could leave her children in the care of skilled child-minders. In dire need, a woman may have to do what Laxmi D. (a friend of Santilata who has not been introduced before) does sometimes:

> Shanti called Laxmi, and she appeared at the door, smiling, curious. She was wearing an old sari, washed a hundred times, and no blouse underneath it. And she looked beautiful, holding herself upright, a proud but gentle young woman.
>
> She brought the only stool from inside the house to the garden and insisted I should sit on it. From somewhere another chair was brought for Shanti. We introduced ourselves and I explained the purpose of this visit. She listened, seemed interested, but she did not ask questions.
>
> ....
>
> "How often in a month do you go out for day-labour?"
>
> "Two or three days in a week; I cannot go more often because I have the baby now."
>
> "What kind of work do you do then?"
>
> "Carrying mud, stones."
>
> ...
>
> "Who looks after your baby when you are away the whole day?"
>
> (She went inside the house to get the baby, a healthy little girl with huge dark eyes)
>
> "I have to leave it here, I leave the children here and lock the door. There is nobody to leave the baby with." She smiled; it was a shy smile, as if asking for understanding and support.

Most of us will be well aware of stories of abandoned children, of street gangs; of murder patrols who set out to 'do away' with these begging and stealing children. Many of these children have mothers, who like Laxmi have no other choice but to leave the children to themselves - or to send them out for child-labour, if they are old enough. In a more ideal world, these mothers would get together, form 'networks', taking turns to look after their children, setting up voluntary crèches, or opening up opportunities for day-mothers and other such facilities. But often it needs an outside intervention to get anything going. Day-to-day squalor and drudgery do not encourage creative ways of solving problems. Also, women mistrust each other; poverty, a permanent 'hand-to-mouth' existence, increases suspicion and ill-will among people, quite the contrary to what some development romantics would like us to believe. It is only when they see a realistic chance for improving their conditions, that women - and men - will come together and work for a common goal.

Child-care facilities, whether organised on a private and voluntary basis or provided by the government or an employer, are essential to giving women fair chances in society. Santilata, Laxmi and all the other women who need to or would like to get out of 'sitting at home idly for much of the day' need positive signals and encouragement from development workers to use existing - or set up or push for new - child-care facilities for their children.

Lesson 5: Teach women a 'marketable' skill

A marketable skill is a skill which enables a person to produce a product or service that other people need and/or want to buy; a skill with which a woman can earn money in a given market situation. The skill of assembling a computer may not be a 'marketable' skill for a woman with small children in a remote village without electricity; but it may be a 'marketable' skill for a woman who lives in an urban slum in Bangalore or Kuala Lumpur.

Mangama S. [who has not been introduced so far] is a very poor widow, who lives in a slum in Bhubaneswar; her only skill - at least the only one that is left in her old age - is to look after children; she has brought up seven of her own, and taken care of many others. Where she lives now, her skill is not marketable. Nobody can afford to employ a women to look after the children; there is no kindergarten or crèche which could employ Mangama S., making use of her skill.

Miriam's skill (apart from sewing) was to realise, that people wanted cold drinks, and to produce that service for people in her neighbourhood.

The four Gambian market women [see at the beginning of chapter three] can produce pancakes and make soft-drinks; but not many people want the type of pancakes and soft-drinks that these women produce, and the women do not have the ability to make use of their skills and switch to another, more sought after, product. Nor do the have the skill to realise, that improving the quality by improving the hygiene would increase the chances of selling their pancakes.

Every human being has a range of, often dormant, natural talents and throughout her life a number of learned skills add to what could be called an enterprise potential. Women, especially poor women, are often unaware of this potential. And so are the people that work for women's development.

The learned skills and acquired knowledge of women and men in any society, but most prevalent in traditional agrarian societies, are to a great extent related to their "gender domains".[5] In many countries girls are disadvantaged in formal education and have, therefore, less chances of learning non-traditional skills and acquiring new, 'modern' knowledge. This affects their choice of activities and income earning chances in later life. Marilyn Carr analysed research papers from Southern African countries[6] and found that women's enterprise activities were confined to a limited number of traditional 'women's activities' - such as textiles, knitting, food processing, basket-making, and tailoring - based on traditional domestic skills learned at home.[7]

While these traditional skills may at one time have been 'female domains' of equal worth to 'male domains', this worth changes in the context of commercialisation and industrialisation. Activities that are based on female skills are primarily time consuming, provide little income, and are not easily upgraded to yield a higher price. But when traditional women's activities are commercialised, when new or more effective techniques or technologies are introduced, the more remunerative part is often taken up by men.[8]

It can be argued, that traditional female skills are in fact practical survival skills, an "invaluable bank of entrepreneurial resources".[9] But do Preeti, Moti or Prabha have such 'banks of resources'? I have watched them, and many other very poor women, performing normal household and other tasks. Yes, these women do have skills: standing on the rim of a well to heave out a bucket full of water is a skill; balancing heavy loads on ones head; making a fire and keeping it going with the very little fuel, so that the one hot meal can be prepared - all these are skills. But none of these skills, which are essential to keep a family going, and may be sufficient in a society based on subsistence farming, can be turned into cash income other than by performing badly paid, unskilled labouring tasks.

What is more, the women's natural abilities and intelligence are all too often buried under the monotony and poverty of day to day life; buried under social norms and rules, that discourage women's development; buried under economic and social structures, that hinder the poor, and especially poor girls and women, from access to other than the most basic, dull, lifeless 'knowledge', if at all, and from access to skills that can earn an income in the women's own, often very narrow, environment. There are positive examples; it can be done; women's natural talents and skills can be employed for the benefit of society and for the women's own livelihood and dignity. I have seen poor, illiterate women getting involved in re-discovering and using natural herbal medicines, natural dyes; women who have become village health workers, social workers, 'bare-foot' doctors and 'chicken doctors'; women repairing tube-wells, building houses and latrines.

But what about skills for self-employment and enterprise? Ujal K., another woman from Orissa who has not been mentioned before, is one of the few poor, rural women I have met, who had learned a non-traditional skill in order to earn money. In what way has it influenced her life; in what way have her new skills helped her to improve her livelihood?

"I was born a girl, so I did not know the ABC of carpentry. When it was decided in the village meeting that I should be sent for training in carpentry, I was dead against it. I was thinking that this type of work will not help me. But I agreed, when I was convinced that I could earn a lot of money with my newly acquired skills.

During the training period, I had a lot of difficulties. My husband would come and create a racket saying that a woman is not supposed to learn carpentry, and beat me. After such incidents took place, Madam [the woman who initiated the whole training] called for a meeting in the village and told my husband that he could be arrested for such behaviour, if she lodges a complaint with the police. My husband got scared and promised that his behaviour would not be repeated. When the training finished, I was confident about my skills.

After the training I stayed at home for one month. During this period I was the target of a lot of comments, and sniggers regarding my carpentry training - what use was it for me? Not able to bear the taunting any more, I went to Mrs. P. [a woman of a local NGO] and told her my plight. She helped me apply for a loan of Rs 6,000 to start something on my own. On that application, I got Rs 2,000 worth of wood; Rs 1,350 for the shed for carpentry work; and the other Rs 2,650 stayed with the bank. This wood was to be used for making doors and windows. Before I could use the wood the bank manager came to visit me and said that as a woman, would it not better if I go into selling dry fish, prawns and so, instead of trying to work in carpentry. I stuck to my guns, and so the rest of the money was released. With this money, I got a number of necessary tools like saw, hammer, anvil, tool to shave wood, axe and so on, as well as two tins of paint.

One day when I was in the process of making a door, our sarpanch [headman of the village] came and asked very dripping with irony whether my hands can carry a saw and hammer, whether I can finish the door I started. In reply, I proceeded to make the door in front of his very eyes, and got Rs 400 for my efforts. I also made a bed, for which I got Rs 100.

Before my success none of the villagers ever called me by name. They used to call me as so-and-so's wife, or so-and-so's mother, or so-and-so's daughter-in-law. Never Ujal K. . Now they ask for me by name: Is Ujal K. there? The Ujal K., the individual with her own identity! Women got their self-respect now!"

Ujal's life has taken a turn for the better; but would she be able to maintain her carpentry business, if the NGO which is supporting her, were to leave or close down? Now she has the protection of Mrs. P. and gets her supplies of timber with the help of the NGO; they also help her to find customers outside her village. When I met her the second time, she agreed to give me some financial details of her carpentry; it turned out that Ujal was probably making a loss, but she did not see it that way; there was cash coming in and she was getting respect; for her the 'business' was successful. With continuous support from the NGO she will probably be able to succeed; she is learning by doing, getting experience and exposure because of her new skills and the support. One day she will be able to be independent.

A skill for a business that is to provide sufficient income is more than the skill to produce a product or service. It must include the skill to sell the product or service; that the buyer might be an NGO is of no importance to the actual need of the woman to acquire that skill. It must include the skill to calculate a remunerative price for it; to find suppliers, customers; to confront and fight harassment by corrupt government officers; it must also include knowledge about adequate equipment and techniques, and about the meaning and importance of 'adding value'.

Must all women, who want to or have to be self-employed, have these skills? The widow Paidama [she has not been introduced before] buys a few limes and chillies in the morning from the main market in Bhubaneswar and sells them on the roadside near her community. From the few Rupees she makes during the day, she buys food and keeps some for the next morning to buy a new supply of limes and chillies. No, for that she does not need the skills mentioned above. Hers is a "survival business"; Paidama lives a hand-to-mouth existence and the hand does not provide much for the mouth, either. She does not have money to repair the door of her two by two meters mud hut she calls her home, where she lives in permanent fear of being assaulted. What kind of skills would she need to increase her income? The skill to "add value"? To make lime juice, or to wax and pack six limes in a plastic bag? Who in her neighbourhood is going to have the money to buy such products? The skill to calculate her costs and prices? If she did a proper calculation of costs and included a minimum wage for herself, her price would be unacceptable to her customers. Or should she be trained in tailoring? No, for a woman like Paidama a loan to buy more limes and other vegetables would be of much more immediate help. It would increase her earnings; not very substantially but enough to improve her condition.

Manimala, Miriam, Bintou, Poonaman, Ujal and Lucy are the women who are earning sufficient money by being self-employed or running a business; all had either a skill or knowledge of how things work, how to approach institutions, banks, customers. The more successful among them where not very poor when they started their enterprise, partly because they already had a skill which enabled them to get employment.

To teach women a skill is to set them on a path that is more likely to lead them out of poverty. Skills and knowledge are needed in every area of life; poor people, especially poor women who have been born into poverty, have little chances to acquire skills and knowledge. Be it issues of birth control, rights, hygiene and nutrition, tending animals, growing healthy plants - all these require specific knowledge and skills, if they are to be done well and effectively. So does enterprise, even if it is to remain 'micro'.

Gaining security

Kuri, Ulash, B.Parmer and Mary earn a fairly regular income by doing wage-work; they are not interested in earning more money through enterprise, because they do not believe that by being self-employed they could earn more. But why do women like Kuri and Ulash have a negative inclination towards enterprise, while other similarly pragmatic women like Kasai or Miriam have a positive inclination?

Miriam has a specific skill with which she can produce products that sell in the market, and Kasai has access to community land where she can grow vegetables, fruits, cash crops. Kuri and Ulash do not have such skills or land. All four of them are the sole or main income earners in their families. But while Kasai has a supportive and encouraging 'development network' and access to land, and Miriam has a husband who earns at least a small, regular income, Kuri has no such network or husband, her children are still young and although two of them contribute a little income this would not feed the family. And Ulash? Her father is very ill, her brother is a drunkard who does not contribute anything, her mother has to look after the father and feels old and weak, and there is no extended family network. Kuri, Ulash, B. Parmer and Mary depend entirely on their wage work.

Employment opportunities for women (and men) in developing economies are scarce; and those available for women are usually badly paid. One could therefore assume, that women would take up any opportunity to become self-employed instead of being under-paid and often humiliated by employers. But the millions of extremely badly paid and mostly female domestic helpers, for example, in every corner of the world, indicate that the relatively secure income is more important to them.

Kuri, Ulash, B. Parmer and Mary's stories tell us that if a woman's family depends on her income which she earns through miserable, badly paid but relatively regular wage-work, she is likely to prefer the security of that work and not to venture into self-employment. Their perception of enterprise is negative, yet it would be wrong to push these women to become 'entrepreneuses'.

So, should we leave these millions of women alone or is there anything we can contribute to their 'empowerment', to their having better wages and more job security? I believe there is; Kuri and the other women have opened my eyes to a large social problem, to which very few of us have given any thought, yet many of us will find it on our doorsteps or even in our own houses: the exploitation of 'maid servants' or domestic helpers.

Lesson 6: *Wage-earning women need 'trade unions'*

I do not believe that it would be easy to convince Kuri or Ulash, and not even Mary from Jamaica, to join some sort of domestic helper's or other women worker's trade union. Like most women, they, too work in the 'informal sector', there is no contract, no registration, no taxes and no social security contributions. They can be hired and fired at a moment's notice; and for every domestic helper there are at least a dozen other women who want her job on any conditions. There is no bargaining power left, then, for women working in these conditions. Joining a union of some sort would only make matters worse, would make these women less employable, for trade unions are perceived as groups of people who agitate and threaten employers.

Would it? Are there circumstances when it would not? Trade unions, says Ela Bhatt, also have another purpose apart from that of agitation: "... to create solidarity among self-employed women and, if need be, to agitate against certain policies as well as certain deficiencies in their implementation".[10] Ela Bhatt's Self Employed Women's Association is a Trade Union with its own bank and a number of cooperatives ranging from rag-pickers to video-producers; domestic helpers are not among them although there must be thousands in Ahmedabad alone, the city where SEWA has its headquarters.

So how to organise domestic helpers, how to communicate with them? They are more scattered than any other group of self-employed women and far more difficult to reach. Those who live in the house of their employer often do not get out at all, or only once in a while to visit their family in some far away village.

I do not know any organisation that organises domestic helpers. But I know that they exist, that there are organisations acting like placement agencies, training women in certain aspects of housekeeping, cooking, how to perform other functions like taking telephone messages and the like. The women thus trained are then assisted to find employment; because of their training - and the certificate they get at the end of the training - they have better bargaining power: they can ask for higher wages and better conditions. Often the agency will also run or organise a social security and pension scheme for these women. And there are enough employers who are willing to pay a higher wage, when they know that they are getting a better service, when they know they can trust the woman they are employing. These services are one attempt to alleviate the problem of exploitation of domestic helpers.

Such a service might reach Mary, because she is likely to listen to the radio where such services can be advertised, or through an information stall at the doorstep of her church. Kuri, though, is much more difficult to reach. She does not listen to the radio, her various employers would think it odd if she did; she does not have a radio, anyhow. Kuri would have had to be reached at a much earlier point in her life; she is tired now, she mistrusts people and is sceptical, to say the least, about change.

There are no 'quick fixes' for the plight of Kuri and Ulash. What can be done immediately, though, is to let the world know about the "hidden lives"[11] of these women, and to be their advocates.

Becoming ambitious

In the previous chapter the typical positive-pragmatic woman was described as a woman who has to earn money and welcomes any opportunity to do so; income for survival and subsistence is the motivating force and not the activity or the enterprise. The difference between Kasai or Sadapili and Naranga is, that Naranga really wants to have her own consumer shop; she is not happy with the women's group shop. Kasai earns most of the family income from farming vegetables and cashew nuts and in her story and our first meetings she was very enthusiastic about the improvements her 'artificial network' had helped her to achieve. Then the silk business came along and she has, together with the other women of her group, has invested a considerable amount of time and effort in this new project, especially in the growing of the new species of mulberry trees. Kasai is, after all, in the first place a farmer, and so are many of the other positive-pragmatic women; this is their world, this is where their experience is. Kasai learned carpentry, like Ujal K., but she sees carpentry as a useful skill to apply at home or to help other people, while Ujal, who has no land, realised the opportunities in setting up a carpentry workshop in her village. Yet even Ujal remains a farmer at heart:

> "I am planning for the future now. It would be good if more women could have carpentry training. With this training, we could form a group and open a workshop from which not only our families, but the whole village would profit. With the money saved in this way, we could buy cows and maintain them. The doors of prosperity would be open for us also!"

And what about the non-rural women like Miriam, Letwin, or Isatou? Why are they not trying hard to make their enterprising activities and micro-enterprises grow and thus earn them a better income? Why did Miriam never start a 'proper' garments business like Poonaman? Because she never thought of her activities as 'business'; they were means to earn the money to keep the family going; any other means would have done, had there been any. In fact, Miriam would much prefer to have had a job. The same applies for

Letwin, who could for example run a market stall like Lucy, to sell her own and other women's rural products, but chooses not to do so.

Miriam and Letwin are among the more fortunate of the positive-pragmatic women: they have a husband who earns and brings his money home. Many positive-pragmatic women are less lucky. Also, many enterprising activities are tedious or produce very little income, there is nothing to be enthusiastic about. Given the poor environment of these women, the poverty of their customers, the limitation of their skills, there is little scope for growth, for earning more than a few rupees or pesos a months, the absolute minimum to survive. What is the use of being ambitious?, these women might ask themselves.

But why are Malati and Bharati ambitious? Malati's situation is not so different from Prabha's. But she has a 'network' of friends in the community; she has a friend who would like to start a groundnut business with her because she knows how to roast groundnuts, she has a skill that seems to be 'marketable'. Also, and very importantly, Malati is free, she is not bound by a husband or children, she can put all her energy in planning and setting in motion her new idea. Bharati, on the other hand, has work experience and contacts and can therefore imagine herself in business. What both women need is money; money to buy a sewing machine, to buy seeds and implements.

What have I learned from all the positive-pragmatic women like Kasai, Isatou, Miriam or Letwin?

- that rural women are farmers at heart;
- that most poor women who are involved in enterprising activities would prefer to have secure employment; and
- that enterprising women need access to money.

All these points are so obvious, that many readers may be somewhat surprised I find them worth mentioning at all. They are 'old hats', we have known these things for many years, for decades. I believe, though, that there are likely to be many development planners and 'experts' like myself, who need to be reminded constantly about basic issues, the basic needs and realities of the people they plan for, work with and write about. It is not only development fashions, but also our own enthusiasm - and our own helplessness - that lead us to propose those solutions to poverty whose implications are easier for us to understand and quicker for us to implement.

Micro-enterprise promotion programmes are a case in point: because it is 'micro', we believe we understand the implications; we believe that micro-enterprise is easy to do, must be easy to do, it's only 'micro' after all; the same goes for micro-credit programmes.

Pushing for, implementing and supporting land reforms, for example, takes much more patience, willingness to confront the powerful, willingness to give up power. Teaching people solid skills, skills that would get them employment, or would enable them to set up enterprises based on more solid foundations takes time, and long-term investments and responsibilities. But it can be done.

On the next pages I shall be discussing briefly two of the lessons I mentioned above. About the third one - that enterprising women need access to money - a great deal is currently being written and many workshops and conferences are being held about this topic.[12] I do not believe it is necessary to add to that. But it may be useful, to summarise here the findings of a study on women's economic empowerment in South Asia",[13] because it makes reference to "credit"; the authors of the study came to the conclusion

- that access to credit is only one form of economic empowerment, increased bargaining power for higher wages and better working conditions can have more far-reaching consequences and affect more women's (and men's) lives;
- that economic empowerment means bringing women into the mainstream of economic activity and reducing their dependence on NGOs;
- that access to credit is usually a necessary condition for women's involvement in productive activities but rarely a sufficient one;
- that it is necessary to work at both the micro and the macro (advocacy) level if significant and sustained change is to be realised;
- that it is important to bring men along and thus reduce conflict at household, workplace and community level;
- and that the most effective entry point to organise women for empowerment is economic empowerment.

Lesson 7: Rural women need land

"The earth provides enough to satisfy every man's need but not every man's greed."

Mahatma Gandhi

*****

Do women really want to be farmers? Do they really want to do the backbreaking labour that goes with working the land? Here's what some rural women from Orissa had to say:

"Now we started planning for the future. We have opened a shop to sell these products. We also are planning to buy two cows. The money obtained from selling milk is to be deposited in the bank. We would like to buy a plough, only if we had a bit of land." (Premamani H.)

"In our village there are twenty-eight families. Our primary occupation is working as coolies. Our daily bread comes from this coolie work. If we do not go to work, we would have to starve. We could be farmers, but half an acre of land is far too little to sustain a family." (Naya J.)

"If we had a small plot of land we could cultivate crops for our kitchen - this is another immediate worry. Our future would be great if this would be achieved." (Phulamani S.)

"The [local government], seeing our difficulties, gave us a bit of land on which we could cultivate fruits and vegetables. This has helped us a lot. Now, I am planning for my children's future. I need a cow to sell milk, and 2 - 3 oxen for agriculture purpose. But to get these, I need money, which I do not have as yet." (Naranga P.)

It is women more than men who produce the world's food: In Africa and Asia up to eighty percent of all agricultural work is done by women; in Latin America more than forty percent. But even in places where agricultural reforms have been successful and land has been redistributed to poorer people, women have only indirectly benefited. I have listened to many stories about of men - husbands and fathers - who for gambling, drink or other women had to mortgage or sell the land that supported them and their families. Sebastiana's husband is one example; Sebastiana G., a woman from Colombia, [who has not been mentioned before] told the following story:

"Some twenty years ago we came to Barranquilla from Antioquia; our three children were small then and we were outsiders, foreigners. It took a long time to make friends with a few people in the community. My husband's cousin's family was my only contact then. The cousin had suggested that we should come here; my husband had to leave his native village, there had been some problems ... I am not sure what... I was so busy with my children and everything else .... We sold our plot of land and came. He said we had to go. I cried a lot at that time, leaving my family and leaving all I had planted with my own hands and seen it grow. No, we did not have a big house like yours, but it was a decent place, with three rooms and there was a spring behind the house with delicious, fresh water.

Well, my husband found a job here with the Cardoso brothers, you know, they have several haciendas. We bought a little plot of land and a small house with the money from Antioquia; old Mr. Cardoso helped us, God bless him, he was one nice man. For some years our life was good again; we were not rich but we had a home and enough food. Our children went to school and later I married my two daughters. Then came the blow: My husband died in an accident and as if that had not been bad enough, men whom I had never seen in my life before came to ask for my husband's debts to be paid. It turned out that during the last year or so of his life he had gambled a lot and had been borrowing money from moneylenders, giving our land and house as security. I realised that this was probably what had driven us away from Antioquia in the first place. I had to sell everything .... luckily by then my daughters were safely married and my son was working as a shop assistant. But look at me now ... I am getting old and have to wash other people's dirty laundry. And my house is a ramshackle place with a tin roof than will be blown off any day by a storm. My son is turning out like his father, what am I to do....?"

No serious development intervention that wants to assist rural women to improve their livelihood, can avoid addressing such fundamental issues as land ownership for women. If cultivable land is what most poor rural women want, land that they own, that their husbands cannot sell for drinking or other women, then more development intervention efforts must be re-directed to help these women to achieve their goal. Research also suggests that an improvement of women's control over land would have a direct impact on women's production and improve the inequalities of food distribution that exists in many South Asian households.[14]

There are positive examples of successful re-distribution of land. No doubt that it is not an easy task, that it takes more than just giving landless women a plot of land and hoping that all is well; that these women (and their families) will need support for a long time. But it can be done!

Lesson 8: Poor women need employment opportunities

With a few exceptions, all the women presented in the previous chapters want employment of some sort. But employment means that somebody has to have the skills and all it takes to make profits which can be reinvested, creating the work places that women want. Or it means that there have to be enough tax-paying people to enable the government to create public sector employment. These are longer-term issues that, so we hope, development planners are addressing in one way or another. For the shorter-term needs of women, the voluntary sector is trying to step in, setting up 'income-generating programmes' for women. It is these programmes that are my immediate concern here.

There appear to be some common features of many of these 'projects'; while many NGOs claim that their income-generating projects belong to, are owned by the women, women are in fact only wage- or piece-rate workers in training-cum-production centres set up these NGOs, or are working from home with raw-materials and designs provided by NGOs, who also market (or store, unsold) their products.

For the women, the main aim is to earn an income; the difference from working for a private 'entrepreneur' - if there would be one to employ them - may be that the NGO is more sympathetic to their needs and may involve them at some stages of the decision making process.

Another, financially more relevant difference is, that while the 'entrepreneur' has business skills and contacts, people managing NGOs usually do not have such experience, are often in fact hostile to 'business'. They see their activities as something that must be done for the benefit of the women, the old 'welfare to women' principle still prevails; the IGP (income generating project/programme) is not seen as something that has to make profits in order to sustain it, in order to develop more skills, to buy better implements, to secure the women's wages on a longer term. And so the women are quickly taught a skill, the organisation acquires the necessary equipment and raw-materials and the women start producing: mats, pickles, embroidery, wall-hangings, dolls, needle-work, knitted materials, pottery, brooms - the list is endless. The products, although often produced for the upper-income end of the market, are mostly of low quality.

Many of the positive-pragmatic women I have met in various countries, work for at least a few hours a week in such 'income-generating programme'. Of the women I have presented in this and the previous chapters, eight have been or are involved in such activities, and Kasai's failed group engagement in silk production (see page 59) is one case in point, as are others, that I have mentioned in chapter one.

Why did Kasai and the other women in her group fail? What could the NGO have done to prevent this? I believe, the women were not 'ready' for this kind of business; they had not been the ones to initiate it (although this is not always a reason for failure) and they were not used to the amount and regularity of work it needed. The life of the people of J. has improved dramatically over the last ten years; the women are contented with what they have now, it is so much better than before. The process of silk production is a complicated one and obviously more than the women were able to manage, not only in actual working hours but also in 'business management' terms. The NGO is keen to bring self-sufficiency to the people, but the people, the women in particular, want security.

The issue is then: should and can NGOs run proper enterprises that employ women, instead of implementing 'projects', that are not really owned by anyone? It is, of course, a complicated issue and not only related to the NGOs' lack of business knowledge. In most countries there are legal reasons against it; NGOs are charitable organisations, enjoying tax-free status and donors are encouraged to make donations, because they can set these against their taxable income. NGOs would lose this tax-free status, if they start making profits, unless they set up a separate entity, which would be subjected to normal business legislation and taxation.

But many NGOs are de facto employing women and it is an issue that needs to be addressed and analysed carefully. By starting 'income generating activities' for women, all manner of misleading messages are given to women, women who are mostly illiterate, inexperienced in any business dealings and with no exposure to the world outside their community. For most women an IGP is a source of income for which someone else is taking responsibility. For most NGOs women's IGPs are 'projects', of a temporary nature, depending on funds from donor agencies, because the products produced cannot pay for the running of the 'project'. It feels good to pay poor, grateful women a few rupees or pesos or dalasis, and to sell their products at bazaars to people who admire the voluntary work and the commitment to the poor. But women need security on a longer term basis, they need more regular income, they need jobs, not projects.

From ambition to success

Why have Malati or Bharati not succeeded in starting the enterprise they are ambitious to set up? The main reason both gave is that they do not have enough money. But is money the only reason why Manimala, Poonaman, Bintou or Lucy are relatively successful? What are the main ingredients of their success?

Bharati, Manimala and Poonaman are in the same line of business: made-to-measure tailoring and ready-made garments. Bharati has not yet started a tailoring business of the kind that Manimala owns. All three women had tailoring skills and work experience when they decided to become self-employed. But while Manimala had an old sewing machine from her uncle, and Poonaman had some savings and a husband earning a regular income, Bharati would have to buy a sewing machine and has no money to do so, nor a husband who earns enough.

Will Bharati ever be successful in the same way as Manimala? Would she be able to earn enough to feed her family and even to buy a few 'luxury' items such as a fan and a TV, as Manimala has done? It is doubtful because Bharati, at least for some time, will not be able to reach the same kind of market as Manimala, and less still as Poonaman. Her market is a very poor neighbourhood and the quality of her stitching is low. Building up enough capital to enable her to shift to, or cater for, a better-off community would be very difficult for Bharati. Manimala can charge seven to nine Rupees for cutting and stitching a blouse, but women in Bharati's community are only willing to pay five Rupees for it. Manimala lives in the centre of a very busy town; Bharati lives in a poor resettlement that is miles away from the city, where it is much more difficult to get access to better-off customers. Manimala is unmarried, independent, without children; she can dedicate any time she likes to her business; what is more, she has a sister who helps her if need be. Bharati has a young family; children, husband, elderly mother-in-law demand much of her time.

And what made Poonaman financially more successful than Manimala? Poonaman's standard of living is much higher than it was twenty years ago when it was probably similar to Manimala's condition today. Will Manimala own a house and a car and all that in, say, fifteen years time? It is to be doubted; not only is society around her poorer than society in Thailand. It is also because an Indian woman will find it more difficult than a woman in Thailand to go round to wholesalers and middlemen to sell her products. Manimala does not, like other, more successful Indian business women, have a male member of the family, who could carry out these 'outside' business dealings for her.

Manimala is slowly growing into being a 'business woman', an 'entrepreneuse'. From several remarks in her story one can conclude, that Manimala did not start her tailoring business because she was ambitious to do so. One or two years back I would probably have categorised her as a positive-pragmatic type of enterprising woman. She had to do it, because her father died. But she gained experience, became confident, gained the confidence of her customers, the income is not bad. Now she is ambitious that her business should grow; she has the potential, but she needs more capital, and she is likely to get another loan from her bank after she has paid back the current one.

Manimala, Poonaman, Lucy and Bintou all had some financial means or adequate equipment when they started their enterprise; all have a specific skill, and work experience; they have the support of their families; they don't have small children to look after or if they have, there is an institution or an extended family network to do it. The combination of these factors helped them succeed. They have gained 'inner strength' from their own self-reliance; they are able to approach a bank, talk to a house- or stall-owner, deal with customers. Apart from a general business environment, and the economic progress of their communities and countries, one important factor that may hinder their further success as business-women is the boundaries of their gender, prescribed by society and imbibed by them so thoroughly - as we have seen in chapter two - that it has become 'nature' to them.

Grace Mumo, who started and runs a very successful bakery business in Kenya, thinks that one great problem about women entrepreneurs, and women in general, is that they do not know their rights and do not appreciate themselves.

For Maznah Hamid, one of the most successful female entrepreneurs in Malaysia, the main obstacles to growth are the women themselves: "They don't want to go top", and "In many situation it is even an advantage to be a woman entrepreneur; people are willing to help, to co-operate - if only one is clear about ones goals". She thinks, that exposure is important for the development of creativity and self-confidence but that women in Malaysia lack exposure.

Lesson 9: Success comes with experience and exposure

Success comes with confidence, and confidence comes with experience and exposure; life experience, work experience, exposure to different ways of life, different ways of doing things. "You need a change of wallpaper" my mother used to say when I complained to her about how I was stuck in some problem. Meaning: you need a change of scenery, exposure to something different or new, to get away from the monotony of every day life. "I need to charge my battery" my husband explained his reason for wanting a one year sabbatical away from home, away from England. I have not seen many people who have *not* gained from a "change of wallpaper", from "charging their batteries" and those few were stuck in the dullness of their class or caste prejudices and expectations.

Exposure to something different is not only relevant for enterprise success, but for any other success a person may be aiming at. Naranga, the tribal woman from Orissa, has been successful in getting involved in politics (she has been elected to the local council). She believes that much of her newly found confidence came from participating in a rally:

> "I went for over a month in a padayatra [rally by walking long distances for a certain purpose; pada = feet, yatra = festival]. After this padayatra I gained a lot of courage and strength. It was after this when one day, when I was selling spinach in the local market, a man came and asked me how many bundles I sell for one Rupee. I replied "four". He then said that he is a policeman and that I should give him four bundles for 50 paise. I asked him to come dressed in uniform and then I will sell him the four bundles. He was taken aback. Gathering courage, I told him that if he acts smart anymore, I will take his pants and shirt off! [shirts and pants are a symbol of oppression; government official wear shirt and pants; local men wear lunghis, a type of sarong] ... We are more confident and courageous than ever before!"

Success in enterprise is often based on work experience. Work experience does not necessarily lead to an enterprise activity which involves the same skills; but a job can be the general learning ground. Manimala and Poonaman are good examples of women who have successfully applied their work experience. Other women start more carefully: A study in the Caribbean, for example, revealed a prevalent strategy of women for entering self-employment; they typically began their career as an employee and used the secure basis of a job to experiment with self-employment.[15]

An old German proverb says that 'travelling educates' (although in the times of mass tourism and package tours to ghetto-beaches this has lost some of its meaning). But travelling is not the only means of exposure; training, demonstrations, meeting people of different race, caste, class, professions, seeing how they do things differently; mass-media like radio, TV and, increasingly, videos and the Internet all have or can have their share in changing people's view of the world and, consequently, their perceptions. These means will have to be brought into villages and poor communities in order to reach women, who are usually, for a whole range of cultural and economic reasons, far more immobile than men.

Women's status and their roles in the family and society allows them only to have limited access to information and training resources. They are unlikely to go outside the village to approach resource persons or to look for information. Men do not find it important to provide women with information; men ignore women's economic roles as heads of households, income earners, farmers and consumers. And women's own lack of self-worth and confidence increases this isolation.[16]

I have discussed the significance of women's groups and networks earlier in this chapter. How important networking is for business growth is well documented.[17] But women have far less chances to form professional networks; as with the negative-pragmatic women who need some sort of union, ambitious women might profit from being connected to a federation or professional group, if only to get technical information and assistance, access to further training, exposure to other people's businesses.

Grace Mumo, the successful Kenyan business woman, believes that many women entrepreneurs are weak on the financial management side of their business; she herself would appreciate more training in management and also in technological aspects; she does not know much about the technical side of her enterprise. "But I am not suitable for class-room training", she said. "I would prefer an exposure programme, something practical."

Mary Kiama, who runs a quite successful, home-based fruit juices business, catering for local hotels and restaurants in Nairobi, was trained and worked as a teacher for several years. Then she had the chance to accompany her husband to Singapore for some time; when she came back, she did not want to be a teacher anymore because her Singapore experience had made her aware how badly teachers were treated in her own country. She decided to go into business; some equipment brought from Singapore enabled her to start right away.

These two women, Grace and Mary, are two middle class women, who ventured into business from a point of relative advantage; they had connections with the right people, they had money to travel, money to buy equipment, they had confidence to talk to other business people, like to the hotel managers who buy Mary's juice. Poorer women do not have that advantage, and that is where they need the support: support to get exposure, to get work experience.

In "Where there is no job", John Grierson[18] describes how especially traditional apprenticeship can offer low-cost, culturally appropriate on-the-job-training for self-employment, because apart from transfer of skills this kind of training offers access to networks of customers and suppliers. Manimala is an example of someone who has successfully made use of traditional apprenticeship.

I come from a family were traditional apprenticeship for generations had been the route to stability and relative wealth. Of course, traditional apprenticeship was more favourable and varied for boys and young men, who could choose selection of trades. Until early this century girls and young women in my family - as in so many other families not only in Germany but also in other European countries - learned to be good housewives and mothers by being sent to richer families, where they were apprentices of a kind, so-called "house-daughters", to be taught not only cooking and household management but also 'refined manners', female crafts like embroidery, and the skills to be a perfect hostess which sometimes included playing the piano.

This route to stability and relative wealth in my family was a slow process, interrupted by destructive wars. Yet the skills and networks acquired through traditional apprenticeship made it possible for the men, and for some women in my family, to find a job or become self-employed, to earn an income, even in difficult times.

The trend in development assistance to poor women is to provide loans and, maybe, short-term training programmes which may be addressing general issues of development (empowerment, leadership, legal aspects, health etc.) or may offer training in specific technical skills. Longer term, institutionalised skills training does exist in most countries but is usually not accessible to poor women, even the younger, more mobile ones. This is a gap that urgently needs to be filled, using local skills and resources. Promoting the local tailors' trade in a comprehensive and gender-sensitive manner (exchange programmes, exhibitions, promotion of an association of professional tailors, professional skills up-grading programmes, and the like) will do much more for Bharati, Manimala or Poonaman and for many other women (and men), not only of the present but of future generations, than short term projects.

Such development efforts are likely to take more time and require more in depth knowledge of local circumstances than most of us 'development experts' (local and expatriate ones) care to have, or can afford to have, because many of our development employers want quick, superficial results. Bharati, Manimala and Poonaman may need loans at some point in their business career, but credit programmes alone, or one-off, two or three weeks 'entrepreneurship development programmes' are cheap and short-sighted development approaches.

"Es mejor prevenir que despues curar" - it is better to prevent than later to cure - is a saying that I learned during my Colombian childhood. It is applicable to many situations, also to development where preventing means providing the resources that give a certain protection from becoming poor or falling back into poverty: solid skills - learned through training *and* experience -, and belonging to a 'network' form an important part of such resources.

Bharati, the tailor-to-be, and Ujal, the carpenter, have learned their skills in short-term training courses; it shows in the quality of their products. Ujal does not belong to a network of carpenters, nor did she have the time to gain experience and build up a network of customers. Her carpentry business is making losses and she does not - yet - have the means to 'getting rid of this poverty' (as one woman of her group said). It remains to be seen whether it ever will. And Bharati? Even if she manages to get a loan through her credit and savings group and start her tailoring business, her chances to be successful are small.

The path from despondency to success, if it is feasible at all, is not a straight and fast one. If the support that is provided along this path consists of plasters, pills and walking sticks, instead of good shoes, healthy food and encouraging company, those who walk on it are not likely to reach.

References and Notes

[1] see Birley and Cromie, 1988

[2] the expression has been used in relation to small business promotion, referring to all the "agencies and organisations specifically designed to advise and assist the small firm"; see Birley and Cromie, 1988

[3] Dowling, 1994, pp.52-53

[4] Kanchan Mathur and Shobhita Rajan (1997, p.73) report similar reactions among participants of their programmes

[5] see Illich, 1982, chapter V; the term indicates that the space (and time) occupied by women and men in a given society is not the same, that "each gender domain has its own landscape and its own rhythm" (p.107, footnote 79). Illich gives various examples from a range of ethnographic studies showing how women's and men's duties, and with these duties, tools, space, time and language, differed in traditional societies and how this difference vanishes with the introduction of "genderless machines".

[6] see Carr, 1990, p.48; the countries are: Zimbabwe, Zambia, Tanzania, Lesotho, Swaziland, Malawi, Botswana

[7] see Carr, 1990

[8] see Fluitman, 1989, p.55

[9] Ramachandran, 1993, p.46

[10] Bhatt, 1995, p.88

[11] "Hidden lives" is the title of a book, a family memoir, by Margaret Forster, 1995; the title refers to the 'unsung' lives of several generations of hard-working women in her family, some of whom had to earn a living as servants

[12] for example the recent "Micro-Credit Summit" in Washington

[13] see Carr, Chen & Jhabvala, 1996

[14] see for example Bina Agarwal, 1994

[15] see Downing, 1991, p.7

[16] Nena Terrell conducted a survey among development practitioners in various African countries and came to the same conclusions as others who have written about women's isolation in Southern Asia; see Terrell, 1993

[17] see Birley, 1985

[18] Grierson, 1997.

5 "Now that our eyes are opening"

Some afterthoughts about women's empowerment

The lessons of the previous chapter are to do in some ways with women's empowerment. They are also to do with men's empowerment, or - more often - men's failed empowerment. We have seen stories of despondency and of success, stories of women, whose husbands beat them, because violence seems to be the way, in which men express their despondency and low self-esteem, and of women, who have involved their husbands in their successful enterprise. We have seen stories of women, whose neighbours despised them and stories of women, who have gained the respect of their whole community. The road from despondency to success in enterprise is not a straight one, nor do I suggest it is the road, that most women can take; but it is a possible road. And during the journey, as a woman becomes more confident, loses her 'fear of freedom', she becomes empowered.

That enterprise has an empowering effect, has been suggested by other studies; one of the more recent ones was carried out by Lucy Creevey in eight countries. She found:

> "Because of an increase in income, especially where this had lasted over a relatively long time, women who participated [in projects supporting small enterprises] felt better about themselves. They were generally more optimistic about their futures and they frequently felt that their family position had improved. They had become more important in the family. Their husbands and relatives consulted them ... Moreover, there is every indication that the changes in outlook and expectation experienced by these women can be passed on to their daughters and may even influence the lives of other women in nearby areas."[1]

Empowerment[2] is a very fashionable word these days:[3] people's empowerment, women's empowerment are much used 'buzz-words'. The idea is, that development programmes should aim at increasing power and control of target- or beneficiary-groups over their own lives, "so that they are in a position to become their own development agents in the future." [4]

This implies that we, the development interventionists, are in control of the circumstances of our lives and can therefore help others to become empowered. It implies that 'we' have recipes, skills, knowledge, tools to show 'them' how to do it. Do we really? What does it mean: to be empowered, to be in control of one's own life?

During a workshop on "empowering women through enterprise" which a colleague and I conducted in India, participants from five countries, after lengthy discussions, came up with various lists of characteristics of an empowered woman. An analysis of these lists showed a process of empowerment. From this process-oriented perspective an empowered woman is a woman who

- realises the situation she is in
- has self-esteem, accepts herself as she is and enjoys being a woman
- is able to say no to parents, husbands and others, and willing to dissent with other people's opinions and propositions
- is willing to accept challenges
- is aware of her rights
- is confident to raise against social and political barriers
- exercises choices, also in her sexual and child-bearing capacity
- is (able and free to be) economically independent
- and is a partner in the decision making process everywhere, i.e. in social, economic and political spheres of society.

Interestingly, but not unexpectedly, the contributions of the different country groups (all from a middle-class background) showed the different stages of women's empowerment in these countries: one important contribution from the Indian and Bangladeshi women was 'awareness of the own situation'; the Kenyan and Sri Lankan women's concern was more with 'awareness of rights' and 'economic independence'; the European women found 'self-esteem and enjoying to be a woman' to be important characteristics; a most interesting contribution came from the all-male (Indian) group: they thought that an empowered woman is one who is able to say no to parents, husband and others.

I do not know many women who are truly empowered in the way described above, not in my own countries nor elsewhere. There are a few promising young women I know, and I have met throughout my life women whom I have admired, because of their independent spirit and the way they were happy in themselves. What had made these women what they were, I do not really know. But I cannot recall one, that was not economically independent, either through her own work or through inheritance. More importantly, though, they seemed to have talents and skills, which they were able to put to some use, which made them 'useful' and respected members of their families and communities, in other people's *and* in their own eyes.

Not all of these women were well-to-do, in fact, many were poor in economic terms (household-income, assets etc.), although not destitute. I believe, that one of the reasons why so many writers and workers in 'development' are particularly fascinated by poor women, is the discovery, that one does not gain strength and self-respect from material wealth alone, that strength and self-respect come when one is free of fear. Another discovery is, that illiteracy does not mean feeble-mindedness or stupidity, but only a lack of factual knowledge - the kind of knowledge that seems to clutter our, the 'experts' minds - but that to learn to read and write is part of the process of losing fear in a world, where the written word reaches every corner of the world, if only on Coca-Cola bottles.

In the stories of the tribal women from Koraput, for example, this importance of losing fear comes out many times. Kausalja J. a young, unmarried woman, is now the main income earner in her family; her father is old and weak, mother and brothers work as coolies:

> "While doing coolie work the contractor cheat us and whatever they give we take that much. As much as the contractor makes us work, we do the work. When revenue officers come to our village, the villagers out of fear give money, cereals, chicken, rice and gifts. Even the forest officers come and take chicken and money from the villagers. We used to think these people to be our gods. ... Today, I am able to talk in front of everyone at home as well as in the village. I took training in making different articles of rope and "mriga" [silken type of jute-like material]. After having learnt this, I work in our village and have started earning thirty five rupees a day. Now we don't have difficulties for food or clothing. Now my condition has changed. I have learnt this new type of work and I have learnt how to study. ... Today I have the strength to talk at home as well as take part in village meetings and say my opinions. I have the capacity to earn also."

Premamani H. is another positive example; within ten years she developed from a shy, fearful woman to be the women's leader in her village, capable and willing to speak up:

"Previously we were very ignorant. We were scared by anybody who wears shirt-pant. ... If anybody would come, we used to hide ourselves inside our houses. We were many times threatened by the forest guards for collecting kendu leaves. Out of fear we had to bribe them. If they are paid one day, they will keep demanding. If we bribe them so, what will we eat! Even so, our fear used to compel us to pay them. Very often they would come to the village to ask for these. Our husbands would offer hospitality and bid them farewell on departure. Even then, we never got rid of the forest guards. There were always more threats. ... Slowly our thinking is changing. We do not want to remain in poverty any longer. We heard that there is an office at S. where they teach how to improve the conditions in the village. We started going there regularly. They also held a lot of meetings, in which we women also took part. We learned in this time that for elimination of poverty the poor people should work together. Now we have got courage."

Another women's leader from another village is Phulamani C.:

"We lived all our lives with fear in our hearts. We felt we were cheated while purchasing things from the shops, cheated in our trades, cheated in our wages. We were paid miserable sum for our goods. That time we had no courage to protest, we suffered silently all the injustice. We women especially were in constant dread of men wearing pant-shirt. We, out of fear and ignorance, used to beg-borrow and pay them whatever they asked for. If not given, they used to threaten us and tell lies to further scare us. ... This has stopped, we are not frightened anymore."

And what was it that changed this situation?, I asked the women:

"You have become women leaders; what made you so strong?"
"Earlier we formed women groups of all the women in a village. The local NGO invited only five to six women for training; the villagers selected those who should go. Later other women in the village then decided that the trained women like myself should be their leaders. I think training gave us confidence."
"But you already had some confidence because you accepted the selection?"
"Yes, maybe."
"If one wants to increase one's income, what is most important?"
"New skills which can earn money." (all women agree)
"But skills do not automatically lead to more income. What else must be there?"

"With the skills one can produce things and sell them, for example selling
cocoons, selling carpentry products on weekly markets. There is a
requirement for everything here."
"What would you recommend other women to do in order to come out of
poverty and dependence?"
"We are also teaching other women to improve their lot. Some women want
to continue to work on their land, some want education. We do a lot of
exchange, of talking to other women in other villages; ... well, there are
some women who do not want to contribute. Earlier we did not have much
strength to talk to government officials, now we do; this is also because of
getting together with other women, other people from outside our villages.
That is important to build strength. Attending meetings and melas [fairs]
like this one [our meeting took place after a tribal women's rally and
exhibition] also gives strength and confidence."

Anees Jung's tells stories of empowered women; there is for example
Lallan Bai, a poor, lower caste woman who says: "I have learnt about our
bodies and why they get sick. I have also learnt about people and about
myself. And I have lost fear." Or Suman Bai who learned that "You have to
first get fearless in your own house, then in your village."[5]
The process of empowerment - where is, where should it be leading to?
Margaret Hall developed two hypothetical profiles, two ideal-types of
women: the subjugated and the empowered women. Among the (ideal)
characteristics of empowered women of this typology the ones I found most
essential are those describing empowered women as women who

"...define their attitudes, values and behaviour in relation to their own real
interests. They have autonomy because they claim their freedom from
existing male hierarchies, whether they live in traditional societies or
modern, industrial societies." They also "...maintain equal-mindedness,
rather than act out roles that merely confront and challenge male
dominance. Empowered women do not aim at being superior to men. They
respond as equals and cooperate in order to work toward the common goal."
And they "... do not retreat from the traditional responsibilities, but rather
forge their own ways of doing things."[6]

Miriam from Colombia, Poonaman from Thailand, Lucy from Kenya,
Bintou from The Gambia, Kasai and Naranga from India have 'forged their
own ways', weaving family, community and business into one whole;
an imperfect whole, yes, no great fortunes and fame to be gained.

But it is something of their own which gives them confidence, control over their lives, self-esteem.

Women like Preeti, Prabha or Helen have still to lose fear and to take control of their own lives, be free to forge their own ways - not ours. Changing perceptions is a two ways affair. When Naranga said "...now that our eyes are opening", my eyes were opening, too.

Women are no better human beings than men, but women have different needs, and different ways of communicating with others. Women's more holistic approach to life, and women's caring pragmatism, which can be taught to men, too, may be what is needed to cure this ailing world from many of its maladies. Now that our eyes are opening, there is hope.

References and Notes

[1]   Creevey, 1996, p.209

[2]   The word power derives from the Latin word 'posse' which means to be able. Power has taken many meanings, one of them is "the ability to do or act"; it also means control, authority, influence, vigour, energy.

[3]   Personally, I do not like the word empowerment. When I translate it into my mother-tongue, German, it has a nasty flavour: the "Ermaechtigungsgesetz" (enabling act; the German Word "ermaechtigen" meaning "to empower") of March 1933 enabled Hitler's National Socialist Party to take absolute power; the people who came to power then were by no means the old elite, the rich, although some of them supported the newly empowered men; millions of ordinary Germans, poor, well-to-do, unemployed, self-employed, men, and women, welcomed the 'peoples' party'.

[4]   see Thomas, 1992, p.118

[5]   Jung, 1994, p.67

[6]   Hall, 1992, p.117.

Appendices

Appendices

Appendix 1: List of the women presented in this book

Name (alphabetical)	Country	Activity	Type*	Chapter/Page first mentioned
B. Parmar	India	cook	Neg.-Pragm.	3/54
Bharati A.	India	tailor	Ambitious	3/76
Bintou S.	Gambia	food-stall	Ambitious	3/71
Elisabeth S.	Germany	various	Pos.-Pragm.	3/63
Guchana P.	India	day-labour	Pos.-Pragm.	3/62
Helen D.	UK	domestic helper	Uncertain	2/39
Isatou F.	Gambia	trader	Pos.-Pragm.	3/63
Kasai J.	**India**	**farming and other**	**Positive-Pragmatic**	**3/56**
Kausalja J.	India	day-labour and other	Pos.Pragm.	5/119
Kuri B.	**India**	**domestic helper**	**Negative-Pragmatic**	**3/48**

* Names printed in bold are the main case stories of the respective types

Name (alphabetical)	Country	Activity	Type	Chapter/Page first mentioned
Lata	India	'retired'	---	1/22
Laxmi D.	India	casual labour	Pos.-Pragm.	4/94
Lucy G.	Kenya	fruit-stall	Ambitious	3/74
Malati S.	India	none	Ambitious	3/70
Manimala T.	**India**	**tailor**	**Ambitious**	**3/67**
Mary C.	Jamaica	domestic helper	Neg.-Pragm.	3/55
Miriam M.	Colombia	tailoring and other	Pos.-Pragm.	3/64
Moti B.	**India**	**housewife**	**Despondent**	**2/27**
Naranga P.	India	agric. labour and other	Ambitious	3/72
Nasma R.	Bangladesh	shop-keeper	Pos.-Pragm.	3/63
Phulamani C.	India	day-labour and other	Pos.-Pragm.	5/119
Poonaman C.	Thailand	ready-made garments	Ambitious	3/73
Prabha B.	India	begging	Despondent	2/31
Preeti A.	India	house-keeping	Despondent	2/32
Premamani H.	India	day-labour and other	Pos.-Pragm.	5/119

Name (alphabetical)	Country	Activity	Type	Chapter/Page first mentioned
Sadapili D.	India	selling liquor/ silk-worm rearing	Pos.-Pragm.	3/62
Sangita	India	housewife	---	1/22
Santilata D.	**India**	**housewife/ casual labour**	**Uncertain**	**2/35**
Sebastiana G.	Colombia	washing clothes	Neg.-Pragm.	4/106
Ujal K.	India	carpenter	Ambitious	4/97
Ulash B.	India	day-labour	Neg-Pragm.	3/53
Urmila D.	India	housewife	Uncertain	2/40
Yanjuke T.	Gambia	chamber maid	Uncertain	2/41

Appendix 2:   Currency conversions

All rates are average rates of the relevant year(s)

£ 1 = 4 Malaysian Ringgit (Mal$)

£ 1 = 50 Indian Rupees (Rs)

£ 1 = 12 Gambian Dalassi (Dal)

£ 1 = 84 Kenyan Shillings (Ksh)

£ 1 =   1.50 US Dollars (US$)

Appendix 3: Bibliography

Agarwal, Bina (1994) *A Field of one's own: Gender and Land Rights in South Asia.* Cambridge University Press.

Ahmed, Sara (1993) 'Gendering the rural environment: Concepts and issues for practice'. Workshop report 11. Anand, Institute of Rural Management (IRMA).

Albee, Alana and K.D. Reid (1992) 'Women and urban credit in Sri Lanka'. *Small Enterprise Development* 3 (1), 52-56.

Alsop, Ruth (1993) 'Whose interests? Problems in planning for women's practical needs'. *World Development* 21 (3), 367-377.

Amis, Philip (1994) Indian urban poverty: Labour markets, gender and shocks. *Journal of International Development*; Vol.6, No.5, 635-643.

Anselm, M. (1991) 'Women entrepreneurs - Agents of social change'. In Proceedings of the ENDEC World Conference on Entrepreneurship and Innovative Change 1991. Singapore, Nanyang Technological University - Peat Marwick Entrepreneurship Development Centre (ENDEC), 458-465.

Ardener, Shirley and Sandra Burman (eds.) (1995) *Money-go-rounds. The importance of rotating savings and credit associations for women.* Oxford, Berg.

Awori, Thelma (1995) 'Training issues: Women in micro- and small-enterprises in Africa'; in Dignard, Louise and Jose Havet (eds.) *Women in micro- and small scale enterprise development.* London, IT Publications, 229-248.

Bakhoum, Ibrahima et.al. (1989) *Banking the unbankable. Bringing credit to the poor.* London, Panos Publications.

Baud, Isa and de Bruijne, G.A. (eds.) (1993) *Gender, small-scale industry and development policy.* London, Intermediate Technology Publications.

Beaumont, Sue, Kamal Singh and Kavil Ramachandran (eds.) (1992) *Development of micro enterprises by women.* New Delhi and Ahmedabad, British Council and Indian Institute of Management.

Beck, Tony (1994) *The experience of poverty. Fighting for respect and resources in village India.* London, IT Publications.

Bennett, Lynn and Mike Goldberg (1993) 'Providing enterprise development and financial services to women - A decade of Bank experience in Asia'. World Bank Technical Paper No. 236. Asia Technical Department Series. Washington, The World Bank.

Berger, Marguerite (1989) 'An introduction'. In Berger, Marguerite and Mayra Buvinic (eds.) *Women's Ventures*. West Hartford/Connecticutt, Kumarian Press.

Bernstein, Henry (1992) Poverty and the poor. In Bernstein, Henry; Ben Crow and Hazel Johnson (eds.) *Rural livelihoods - Crises and responses*. Oxford and Milton Keynes, Oxford University Press in association with The Open University, 13-26.

Bhatt, Ela (1988) 'Women and small-scale enterprise development in a new era'. Remarks presented to the International Institute of Development, Ottawa; reprinted in Background Papers, Symposium on Expanding income earning opportunities for women in poverty: A cross regional dialogue. Nairobi, The Ford Foundation.

Bhatt, Ela (1995) 'Women and development alternatives: Micro- and small-scale enterprises in India'; in Louise Dignard and Jose Havet (eds.) *Women in micro- and small scale enterprise development*. London, IT Publications, pp.85-99.

Bhatty, Z. (1987) 'Economic contribution of women to the household budget: A case study of the beedi industry'. In Menefee Singh, A. and A. Kelles-Viitanen *Invisible hands. Women in the home-based production*. New Delhi, Sage.

Bird, Barbara (1989) *Entrepreneurial behavior*. Glenview, Ill.: Scott, Foresman and Co.

Birley, Sue (1985) 'The role of networks in the entrepreneurial process'. *Journal of Business Venturing* 1, 107-117

Birley, Sue; Caroline Moss and Peter Saunders (1987) 'Do women entrepreneurs require different training? *American Journal of Small Business*. Summer 1987, 27-35.

Birley, Sue (1988) 'Female entrepreneurs - Are they really different?'. Working paper 5/87. Cranfield School of Management.

Birley, Sue and Stan Cromie (1988) 'Social networks and entrepreneurship in Northern Ireland'. Paper presented at the Enterprise in Action Conference, Belfast, September 1988.

Boserup, Ester (1970) *Women's role in economic development*. London, Georg Allen & Unwin.

Bossen, Laurel (1975) 'Women in modernizing societies', as quoted in Frauen in der Dritten Welt. *Blaetter des IZ3W*, 87, 19-27.

Bruce, Judith (1988) 'A home divided: Women and income in the Third World'. Background Papers, Symposium on Expanding Income Earning Opportunities for Women in Poverty. Nairobi, The Ford Foundation.

Bumiller, Elisabeth (1990) *May you be the mother of a hundred sons. A journey among the women of India*. New Delhi, Penguin Books.

Buvinic, Mayra (1986) 'Projects for women in the Third World: Explaining their misbehavior'. *World Development*, 14 (5), 653-664.

Buvinic, Mayra and Nadia Youssef (1978) 'Women headed households: The ignored factor in development planning'. Report prepared for USAID, Office of Women in Development. Washington, D.C.: International Center for Research on Women.

Canadian International Development Agency (CIDA) (1986) 'Women in development and the project cycle: A workbook'. Draft January 1986. Hull, CIDA.

Carr, Marilyn (1984) *Blacksmith, baker, roofing-sheet maker. Employment for rural women in developing countries*. London, IT Publications.

Carr, Marilyn (1990) 'Women in small-scale industries- some lessons from Africa'. *Small Enterprise Development*, 1 (1), 47-51.

Carr, Marilyn; Martha Chen and Renana Jhabvala (eds.) (1996) *Speaking out. Women's economic empowerment in South Asia*. London, IT Publications.

Carter, Sara and Tom Cannon. (1988) 'Female entrepreneurs. A study of female business owners; their motivations, experiences and strategies for success'. Research paper no. 65 Department of Employment.

Chambers, Robert; N.C. Saxena and Tushaar Shah (1989) *To the hands of the poor. Water and trees*. London, Intermediate Technology Publications

Chambers, Robert (1988) Poverty in India: Concepts, research and reality. Discussion Paper 241, IDS, University of Sussex.

Chandrasekar, Rajkumari (ed.) (1992) *Women's resource and national development. A perspective*. New Delhi, Gaurav Publishing House.

Chandra, Shanta Kohli (1991) *Development of women entrepreneurship in India. A study of public policies and programmes*. New Delhi, Mittal Publications.

Chen, Martha Alter (1986) *A quiet revolution. Women in transition in rural Bangladesh*. Dhaka, BRAC Prokashana.

Cloud, Kathleen (1985) 'Women's productivity in agricultural systems: Considerations for project design'. In Overholt, Catherine et.al. (eds.) *Gender roles in development projects. A case book.* West Hartford, Connecticut., Kumarian Press.

Creevey, Lucy (1996) *Changing women's lives and work. An analysis of the impacts of eight microenterprise projects.* London, IT Publications.

Cromie, S. (1986) 'Towards a typology of female entrepreneurs'. Paper presented to the Ninth National Small Firms Policy and Research Conference, Gleneagles.

Cromie, Stan and Sue Birley (1992) 'Networking by female business owners in Northern Ireland'. *Journal of Business Venturing* ,7, 237-251.

Crowley, Helen and Susan Himmelweit (1992) *Knowing women. Feminism and knowledge.* Cambridge and Milton Keynes, Polity Press in association with The Open University.

Deka, Phani and A.R.Baruah (1992) 'Women entrepreneurs - challenges and expectations. A study in North Eastern Region.' *Asian Entrepreneur,* 2 (2), 25-32.

Desai, Neera and Maithreyi Krishnaraj (1990) *Women and society in India.* Delhi, Ajanta Publications.

Dignard, Louise and Jose Havet (eds.) (1995) *Women in micro- and small-scale enterprise development.* Boulder, Westview and London, IT Publications.

Dowling, Colette (1994) *The Cinderella complex. Women's hidden fear of independence.* London, HarperCollins.

Downing, Jeanne (1991) 'Gender and the growth of micro-enterprise'. *Small Enterprise Development,* 2(1), 4-12.

Eigen, Johanna (1992) 'Assistance to women's businesses - evaluating the options'. *Small Enterprise Development,* 3 (4), 4-14.

El-Namaki, M.S.S.; J. Gerritsen and C.Beyer (1986) 'Women entrepreneurship revisited; in search of pertinent entrepreneurial traits'. RVB Research Papers VI (1). Delft, Research Institute for Management Science, 3-13.

Eppstein, Scarlett (1988) 'Female petty-entrepreneurs and their multiple roles'. Paper presented at the International Conference on Rural Entrepreneurship, Silsoe College UK, September 1988.

Evans, Judith (1995) *Feminist theory today.* An introduction to second-wave feminism. London, Sage.

Farbman, Michael (ed.) (1981) *The PISCES Studies: Assisting the smallest economic activities of the urban poor.* Washington D.C., Office of Urban Development, Bureau for Science and Technology, U.S. Agency for International Development.

Farbman, Michael and William F. Steel (1992) 'Research issues for small enterprise development'. *Small Enterprise Development,* 3 (2), 26-34.

Feldstein, Hilary Sims and Susan Poats (eds.) (1990) *Working together: Gender analysis in agriculture.* West Hartford, Conn., Kumarian Press.

Finney, Ruth (1977) 'Towards a typology of women entrepreneurs: Their business ventures and family life'. Entrepreneur Development Report; an occasional publication. Honolulu, East-West Centre.

Fischer, E.M.; A.R. Reuber and L.S. Dyke (1993) 'A theoretical overview and extension of research on sex, gender, and entrepreneurship'. *Journal of Business Venturing,* 8(2), 91-180.

Fluitman, Fred (ed.) (1989) *Training for work in the informal sector.* Geneva, International Labour Office.

Fong, Monica S. and Heli Perrett (1991) *Women and credit. The experience of providing financial services to rural women in developing countries.* Milan, Finafrica Foundation.

Forster, Margaret (1995) *Hidden lives. A family memoir.* London, Penguin Books.

Fromm, Erich (1984) *The fear of freedom.* London, ARK Paperbacks.

Fuglesang, Andreas and Dale Chandler (1988) *Participation as process. What can we learn from Grameen Bank, Bangladesh.* Oslo, Norwegian Ministry of Development Cooperation (NORAD).

Gallin, Rita S. and Anne Ferguson (1993) 'The plurality of feminism: Rethinking "difference"'. In Gallin, R.S.; A. Ferguson and J. Harper (eds.) *The Women And International Development Annual,* Vol.3. Boulder, Westview Press, 1-16.

Ghosh, Jayati and Krishna Bharadwaj (1992) 'Poverty and employment in India'. In Bernstein, H. et.al. (eds.) *Rural livelihoods. Crises and responses.* Oxford: Oxford University Press in association with The Open University, 139-164.

Gibb, Alan (1987) 'Stimulating new business development'. In Making small enterprise more competitive through more innovative entrepreneurship development programs. Proceedings of the 1st Asia-Pacific Symposium on Small Enterprise and Entrepreneurship Development; Bangkok and Manila, Technonet Asia, February 1987, 56-69.

Goffee, Robert and Richard Scase (1985)   *Women in charge - The experience of female entrepreneurs.* London, George Allen & Unwin.

Goodale, Gretchen (1989) 'Training for women in the informal sector- The experience of the Pathfinder Fund in Latin America and the Caribbean'. In Fluitman, Fred (ed.) *Training for work in the informal sector.* Geneva, International Labour Office, 179-188.

Government of India (1981) 'Women's activities in Rural India. A study based on National Sample Survey'. Department of Statistics, June 1981.

Grierson, John P. (1997) *Where there is no job. Vocational training for self-employment in developing countries.* St.Gallen, SKAT.

Gupta, S.K. (1990) 'Entrepreneurship development training programmes in India'. *Small Enterprise Development,* 1 (4), 15-26.

Hall, Eve (1988) 'The Port Sudan small-scale enterprise program'. *SEEDS* No.11. New York, SEEDS.

Hall, C. Margaret (1992) *Women and empowerment. Strategies for increasing autonomy.* Washington, Hemisphere Publishing Co.

Harper, Malcolm (1984) *Small business in the Third World.* Chichester, John Wiley & Sons.

Harper, Malcolm and Shailendra Vyakarnam (1988) *Rural enterprise. Case studies from developing countries.* London, Intermediate Technology Publications.

Henshall Momsen, Janet (1991) *Women and Development in the Third World.* London, Routledge.

Hertz, Leah (1986) *The Business Amazones.* London, May.

Heyzer, Noeleen (1993) 'Gender, economic growth and poverty'. *Focus on Gender,* 1 (3), 22-25.

Hilhorst, Thea and Harry Oppenoorth (1992) *Financing women's enterprise. Beyond barriers and bias.* Amsterdam, Royal Tropical Institute together with IT Publication, London and UNIFEM, New York.

Hisrich, Robert D. and Candida Brush (1983) 'The woman entrepreneur: Implications of family, education and occupational experience'. In Frontiers of entrepreneurial research 1983. Wellesley, Mass., Babson College, 255-270.

Illich, Ivan (1983) *Gender.* London, Marion Boyars Publishers.

Iyer, Lalitha (1991) *Women entrepreneurs. Challenges and stategies.* New Delhi, Friedrich Ebert Stiftung.

Jhabvala, Renana and Jane Tate (1996) Out of the shadows: Homebased workers organize for international recognition. *SEEDS* No.18.

Jiggins, Janice (1988) 'Conceptual Overview: How poor women earn income in rural Sub-Sahara Africa and what prevents them from doing so'. In Background Papers, Symposium on Expanding Income Earning Opportunities for Women in Poverty: A Cross Cultural Dialogue. Nairobi, The Ford Foundation.

Jumani, Usha (1991) *Dealing with poverty. Self-employment for poor rural women*. New Delhi: Sage Publications.

Jumani, Usha; Harvinder Bedi and Vasantha Kannabiran (1991) 'Sector survey for training needs assessment'. Draft report for Women's Enterprise Management Training Outreach Programme (WEMTOP). Washington, Economic Development Institute.

Jung, Anees (1987) *Unveiling India. A woman's journey*. New Delhi, Penguin Books.

Jung, Anees (1994) *Seven sisters. Among the women of South Asia*. New Delhi, Penguin.

Kanitkar, Ajit and Jose Sebastian (1993) 'Search for business ideas: A study of successful women entrepreneurs'. Working Paper 46; Institute of Rural Management, Anand.

Karl, Marilee (1995) *Women and empowerment. Participation and decision making*. London, Zed Books.

Keeling, Ann (1993) 'WID in Pakistan'. *Women's Network Newsletter* No.2, Oct/Nov 1993; The British Council, 3-5.

Kraus-Harper, Uschi (1991) 'Entrepreneurship development for enterprising women?'. *Small Enterprise Development*, 2 (1), 42-45.

Kraus-Harper,Uschi and Malcolm Harper (1992*) Getting down to business. A manual for training businesswomen*. London, Intermediate Technology Publications.

Kraus-Harper, Uschi (1992) 'What makes poor women start micro-enterprises?'. In Beaumont, S., K. Singh and K. Ramachandran, *Development of micro enterprise by women*. New Delhi and Ahmedabad, The British Council and Indian Institute of Management.

Kreditanstalt für Wiederaufbau (1990) 'Frauenrelevante Fragestellungen bei Vorhaben der Finanziellen Zusammenarbeit'. Arbeitshilfen-Materialien-Diskussions-beitraege No.1/90. Frankfurt, Auslandssekretariat B, Kreditanstalt fuer Wiederaufbau.

Lloyd, Genevieve (1993) *The man of reason - 'male' and 'female' in western philosophy*. London, Routledge.

Longwe, Sarah Hlupekile (1991) 'Gender awareness: the missing element in the Third World development project'. In Wallace, Tina with Candida March (eds.) *Changing perceptions. Writings on gender and development.* Oxford, Oxfam, 149-157.

Malhotra, Neena (1987) 'Women Entrepreneurship Development in India, with special reference to the role of NAYE'. In Making small enterprises more competitive through more innovative entrepreneurship development programmes. Proceedings, 1st Asia-Pacific Symposium on Small Enterprise and Entre-preneurship Development, Bangkok and Manila. Singapore, Technonet Asia, 114-118.

Mathur, Kanchan and Shobhita Rajan (1997) 'Gender Training: Potential and Limitations'; *Indian Journal of Gender Studies*, Vol.4, No.1, 67-75.

Massiah, Joycelin (ed.) (1993) *Women in developing economies: Making visible the invisible.* Oxford, Berg.

Mayoux, Linda (1993) 'Gender inequality and entrepreneurship: the Indian silk industry'. *Development Policy Review*, 11 (4), 413-426.

Menefee Singh, Andrea and Anita Kelles-Viitanen (1987) *Invisible hands. Women in the home-based production.* Women and the household in Asia; Vol. 1. New Delhi, Sage.

Morgan, David H. J. (1981) 'Men, masculinity and the process of sociological inquiry'. In Roberts, Helen *Doing feminist research.* London, Routledge & Kegan Paul, 83-113.

Moser, Caroline O.N. and Caren Levy (1990) 'A theory and methodology of gender planning: Meeting women's practical and strategic needs'. In Reader, Women in Development. Amsterdam, Royal Tropical Institute, 1-19.

Noponen, H. (1987) 'Organising women petty traders and home-based producers: A case study of Working Women's Forum, India'. In Menefee Singh, A. and A. Kelles-Viitanen (eds.) *Invisible hands. Women in the home-based production.* New Delhi, Sage.

Olivier, Christine (1989) *Jokastes Kinder. Die Psyche der Frau im Schatten der Mutter.* Muenchen, dtv.

Otero, Maria and Elisabeth Rhyne (eds.) (1995) *The new world of microenterprise finance. Building healthy financial institutions for the poor.* London, IT Publications.

Pandey, Sashi Ranjan (1991) *Community action for social justice. Grassroots organisations in India.* New Delhi, Sage.

Piza Lopez, Eugenia and Candida March (1991) 'Gender considerations in economic enterprise'. Report of a workshop in the Philippines. Oxfam Discussion Paper No.2. Oxford, Oxfam.

Poelchau, Susanne (1986) 'Über die 'Sparclubs' der Frauen in Kenya'. *Blätter des IZ3W*, 131/86, 33-36.

Price, Courtney and Stuart Monroe (1992) 'Educational training for women and minority entrepreneurs positively impacts venture growth and development'. In *Frontiers of Entrepreneurship Research 1992*. Babson Park, Mass., Babson College, 216-230.

Purao, Prema; Vrinda Pai; Medha Samant and Mira Savara (1990) *Courage in living. Annapurna women tell their own life stories*. Bombay, Annapurna Mahila Mandal.

Ramachandran, K. (1993) 'Poor women entrepreneurs - lessons from Asian countries'. *Small Enterprise Development*, 4 (1), 46-49.

Rao, Aruna; Mary B. Anderson and Catherine A. Overholt (1991) *Gender analysis in development planning*. West Hartford, Conn., Kumarian Press.

Rashid, Raka (ed.) *Women in local markets and commercial areas. A report and handbook*. PACT Bangladesh.

Reiter, Rayna R. (ed.) *Toward an anthropology of women*. New York, Monthly Review Press.

Risseeuw, Carla (1987) 'Organisation and disorganisation: A case study of women coir workers in Sri Lanka'. In Menefee Singh, A. and A. Kelles-Viitanen (eds.) *Invisible hands. Women in home-based production*. New Delhi, Sage.

Rünger, Helga (1989) 'Wie kann Frauenarbeit bewertet und erleichtert werden?' *Entwicklung und Zusammenarbeit* 12/89, 8-9.

Seager, Joni and Ann Olson (1986) *Women in the world. An international atlas*. London, Pan Books.

Sebstad, Jennefer (1982) 'Struggle and development among self-employed women'. A report on the Self Employed Women's Association Ahmedabad, India. Washington D.C.: Office of urban Development, Bureau for Science and Technology, USAID.

Self Employed Women's Association (1991) 1990 - SEWA Self Employed Women's Association. Ahmedabad: Mahila SEWA Trust.

Shabbir, Amama (1993) 'Women in business: Experiences of women entrepreneurs and non-starters from Pakistan. M.Phil Thesis, Cranfield School of Management.

Shah, Hina (1983) 'Entrepreneurship development in developing countries: Women - the Gujarat experience'. Paper presented at the International Workshop on Entrepreneurship Development. Ahmedabad, November 1983.

Shah, Hina (n.D.) 'Fostering women entrepreurship - A study of distinctive features'. NIESBUD Research Report Serial 3. New Delhi, NIESBUD.

Shapero, A. and L. Sokol (1982) 'The social dimensions of entrepreneurship'. In Kent, Sexton and Vesper (eds.) *Encyclopedia of entrepreneurship*. Englewood Cliffs, NJ, Prentice Hall.

Shastri, Madhu (1990) *Status of Hindu women*. Jaipur, RBSA Publishers.

Sinha, Frances (1983) 'Women, work and technology in rural South Asia'. Occasional Papers 9. London, IT Publications.

Singh, K.P. (1993) 'Women entrepreneurs: Their profile and motivation'. *The Journal of Entrepreneurship*, 2 (1), 47-58.

Smyth, Ines (1993) 'Gender inequality - labour market and household influences'. In Baud, I.S.A. and G.A. de Bruijne (eds.) *Gender, small-scale industry and development policy*. London, IT Publication.

Snyder, Margaret (1990) 'Women, the key to ending hunger'. The hunger project papers no. 8. New York, The Huner Project.

Terrell, Nena (1993) 'Training materials - examining their effectiveness'. *Small Enterprise Development*, 4 (1), 49-52.

The British Council (1993) 'Women's issues in developing countries'. Development priorities: guidelines.

Thomas, Alan (1992) 'Non-governmental organizations and the limits to empowerment'. In Wyuts, Marc; Maureen Mackintosh and Tom Hewitt (eds) *Development policy and public action*. Oxford, Oxford University Press in association with The Open University.

Tovo, Maurizia (1991) 'Microenterprise among village women in Tanzania'. *Small Enterprise Development*, 2 (1),20-31.

Van der Wees, Catherine and Henny Romijn (1987) 'Entrepreneurship and small enterprise development for women in developing countries - An agenda of unanswered questions'. Draft discussion paper based upon research. Geneva, International Labour Office.

Wallace, Tina with Candida March (eds.) (1991) *Changing perceptions. Writings on gender and development*. Oxford, Oxfam.

Wall Street Journal (1994) 'In developing world, international lenders are targeting women'. June 22/94.

Werlhof, Claudia von (1991) *Was haben die Hühner mit dem Dollar zu tun? Frauen und Ökonomie.* München, Verlag Frauenoffensive.

World Bank (1991)   *Gender and poverty in India.* World Bank Country Study. The World Bank, Washington D.C.

Young, Kate (1993) *Planning development with women. Making a world of difference.* London, Macmillan.

Yunus, Muhammad (ed.) (1991) *Jorimon and others. Faces of poverty.* Dhaka, Grameen Bank (3rd. ed.).

For Product Safety Concerns and Information please contact our EU
representative GPSR@taylorandfrancis.com Taylor & Francis Verlag GmbH,
Kaufingerstraße 24, 80331 München, Germany

Printed and bound by CPI Group (UK) Ltd, Croydon, CR0 4YY

08/05/2025
01864391-0003